Preface

Many people in the West have recently evinced considerable interest in the teaching of the Buddha as a philosophy of life answering their practical needs whilst living in a highly industrialized society. In spite of this implied demand for books catering for their requirements, the resultant supply has not come up to expectations.

Numerous books on Buddhism in general have been published in this country but none have, to date, really answered the call for a straightforward approach to the Dhamma (the Buddha's teaching) of a non-scholastic nature and at a price to suit every pocket.

I have, therefore, endeavoured in this volume to present the teaching shorn of accretions, which tend to obscure the real meaning of what the Buddha was getting at, and keeping terminology down to an absolute minimum. I have tried to show that Buddhism does not fit any of the standard definitions, such as 'religion', 'philosophy', 'system of ethics', and the like, but rather that it is somehow a synthesis of all these plus something peculiar to itself. 'Mental training', 'watching the mind' or just plain 'meditation' has come in for quite a lot of attention in recent years, hence any introductory work on Buddhism would be incomplete without some mention of this facet of the Dhamma which is considered, in any case, to be indispensable for its real understanding.

This present work is intended primarily for the Western student who knows next to nothing of the subject but who earnestly wants to glean some knowledge of it by means of a compact, self-sufficing volume which will, nevertheless, not fail to describe the fundamental and unique doctrines of Buddhism in detail.

If this modest work is able to encourage further study and practice, then my efforts will have been amply rewarded.

My sincere thanks are due to Mrs Irene R. Quittner and Mr Russell B. Webb, Chairman and General Secretary of the British Mahabodhi Society respectively for their valuable assistance in various ways to complete this work.

H. S.

First published in Great Britain by George Allen & Unwin 1971
Second impression 1975
Re-issued 1985

George Allen & Unwin (Publishers) Ltd
40 Museum Street, London WC1A 1LU, UK

George Allen & Unwin (Publishers) Ltd
Park Lane, Hemel Hempstead, Herts HP2 4TE, UK

George Allen & Unwin Australia Pty Ltd
8 Napier Street, North Sydney, NSW 2060, Australia

© George Allen & Unwin Ltd 1971, 1985

ISBN 0 04 294071 0

Printed in Great Britain by
Thetford Press Limited, Thetford, Norfolk

The Buddha's Way

H. Saddhatissa, M.A., Ph.D.
Tripiṭakācārya, Paṇḍita

London
GEORGE ALLEN & UNWIN
Boston   Sydney

Works by the same author

Saral-Pāli-Śikṣā
Mahabodhi Society of India
Sarnath, Benares, 1948

Handbook of Buddhists
Mahabodhi Society of India
Sarnath, Benares, 1956

Upāsakajanālaṅkāra
A Critical Edition and Study,
Pali Text Society, London, 1965

Pāli Tipiṭaka Concordance
Volume III, Parts II, III, IV
Pali Text Society, London, 1968–70

Buddhist Ethics
Essence of Buddhism,
George Allen & Unwin Ltd.,
London, 1970

The Buddha's Way

Contents

Illustrations

Abbreviations

PTS indicates issues of the Pali Text Society, London

A.   *Aṅguttaranikāya*, Vol. I, ed. R. Morris, 2nd edn., 1961, V, ed. E. Hardy, reprint, 1959, PTS

Dh. *Dhammapada*, ed. Sūriyagoḍa Sumaṅgala, 1914, PTS

D.   *Dīghanikāya*, Vol. II, ed. T. W. Rhys Davids and J. Estlin Carpenter, reprint, 1947, PTS

M.   *Majjhimanikāya*, Vol. I, ed. V. Trenckner, reprint, 1964, PTS

S.   *Saṃyuttanikāya*, Vols. I–V, ed. Feer, reprint, 1960, PTS

Skt. Sanskrit

v.   verse

vv.   verses

Introduction

There are two modes of thinking, two poles by which one can orientate one's life: politics and religion.

By politics we mean any code of behaviour that implies a classification of men into two or more groups—this classification may be numerical, racial, economic, cultural, and so forth—and thence the superiority of one group over another. An example of altruistic political thinking is the axiom 'The greatest good of the greatest number'. A possibly more realistic approach is typified in the maxim 'He who pays the piper calls the tune'. One of the cruder expressions of political thinking is racial intolerance, one of its more controversial manifestations being the Greek city state where art and freedom flourished against a backcloth of degradation and slavery.

Religious thinking, on the other hand, should be such as to free the mind from the narrowing effects of dogmas usually associated with the word 'religion'. As Milton wrote: 'Let truth and falsehood grapple; whoever heard truth put to the worse in a free and open encounter?'. Two millenia earlier, the Buddha stressed complete freedom of thought without which no truth or insight can result and no effort be exerted: 'Do not go upon what has been acquired by repeated hearing; nor upon tradition; nor upon rumour; nor upon what is in a scripture; nor upon an axiom; nor upon specious reasoning; nor upon a bias towards a notion that has been pondered over; nor upon another's seeming ability; nor upon the consideration, "The monk is our teacher". When you yourselves know: "These things are good; these things are not blamable, these things are praised by the wise; undertaken and observed, these things lead to benefit and happiness", enter on and abide in them.'[1]

In order to live in the world, a working hypothesis incorporating elements from both these modes of thinking is necessary. Different ages, different races, different individuals have weighed the scales more heavily in favour of one or the other.

It is because we feel that many people are now beginning to be sickened by political thinking—and by religious revivals that are political in their aims and/or methods—that we have compiled this book. It is an attempt to present to the Western reader the ethico-philosophical aspect of Buddhism, pruned of the political overtones it has acquired over the centuries. Our aim is not to convert the reader to Buddhism, but only to encourage him in his search for a valid and vital religious basis on which to construct his life.

[1] A., I, p. 189 f.

Part One
Basic Principles

I
Life and teaching of the Buddha

The first point to which attention must be called, if confusion is to be avoided in discussing Buddhism, is that the Buddha at no time claimed to be anything other than a human being. His teaching revolves around the problem of human suffering, and points a way whereby, it is claimed, man can solve this problem— without the aid of any external or supernatural force.

Buddha, meaning one who is enlightened or awakened, was the descriptive name given to an Indian prince, Siddhārtha Gautama, after he had attained a state of complete understanding. It is to a similar state of understanding—and to the freedom from fear and suffering that such understanding brings—that the Buddhist path purports to lead.

Buddhism began in the northern provinces of India, and at one time prevailed throughout Asia. During twenty-five centuries it has mingled with the traditional beliefs of many lands. In modern times there are well over 500 million Buddhists in India, Nepal, China, Japan, Korea, Tibet, Cambodia, Laos, Viet-Nam, Malaysia, Burma, Thailand and Ceylon; and there is evidence of growing interest in America and Europe.

Siddhārtha Gautama is said to have been born in May 563 BC on the day of the full moon in a place called Lumbini Garden close to the northern borders of India. His father, Suddhodana, was ruler of the Sākya country, a kingdom at the foot of the Himālayas. (One of the many names by which Gautama was later to be known was Sākya Muni—the wise man of the Sākyas.) His mother's name was Mahāmāyā.

Many miraculous tales have arisen concerning the birth of the child and his early development. Such tales seem to be one of the occupational hazards of religious leaders. The most modest accounts state merely that after an exemplary childhood he became a youth of noble bearing, combining the skill of the athlete with the intellect of the scholar. In his sixteenth year he married his cousin, a princess of great beauty named Yasodharā. Thirteen years later a son, Rāhula, was born.

The story of how, at the age of twenty-nine, Siddhārtha Gautama left his home, his young wife, and his newborn child, and set out to lead the life of a wandering monk, has, over the years, become tangled in myth and legend. Again we shall give the most simple account. For nearly thirty years the young man had lived a sheltered and probably quite luxurious life. His family was wealthy and seemingly cultured; and he was encouraged to pursue whatever physical or intellectual diversions attracted him. He enjoyed all those comforts and securities that are sometimes said to bring happiness. Yet, from time to time, he was troubled by the sickness and misery he saw around him, and he came to suspect that his way of life was empty. He sought the advice of those who enjoyed a great reputation for wisdom, only to find that they had no adequate answers to his questions.

The course which, in his uneasiness of mind, Siddhārtha Gautama decided to follow—to renounce the world and live as a penniless ascetic—may seem dramatic and perhaps irresponsible today. In the India of six centuries before Christ, it was an extreme but not unusual choice. What makes the case of Gautama worthy of study is not that he chose to renounce the ways of the world but that in his ceaseless quest for the cause and cure of human anxiety and tension he went on to renounce the ways of asceticism as well.

At first his approach was quite orthodox; he consulted priests of the highest authority in the Brahmanic religion of his people—yet none could explain or instruct to his satisfaction. At that time it was the custom to practise bodily mortification in order to gain release from the ills of body and mind; so he tried this method also. In the forest of Uruvela near Gaya he practised the severest austerities for six years and was finally brought near to the point of death.

Suddenly he realized that instead of promoting peace and mental clarity, severe self-imposed penance had ruined his health and dulled his mind. Much to the disgust of his fellow-ascetics, he resolved to reject the ways of austerity just as he had rejected the ways of luxury and to follow instead a middle way between the two extremes. After refreshing his body with food, he sat down under a tree and began to meditate. Right through the night he continued his intensive concentration and by morning he had realized 'two things' which were to be the foundation of his teaching—the truth of the existence of suffering, and the truth that a means of release exists. A middle way avoiding extremes. He spent the remaining forty-five years of his life as an itinerant monk expounding this middle way to all who sought his counsel.

The Buddha's teaching began at Benares, the holy city of the Hindus, to which place he had come immediately following his 'enlightening' experience. Just outside the city, in the deer park at Sarnath, his first discourse or sermon—known as 'The turning of the wheel of the law'—was given. In it was set down in simple terms the fourfold structure of his teaching, usually translated as 'The four noble truths'. They are:

1. The truth that unhappiness exists.
2. The truth that there is a cause for that unhappiness.
3. The truth that unhappiness can cease.
4. The truth of the way that leads to the cessation of unhappiness.

We shall go into some of the details and implications of these 'four noble truths' in later chapters of this book.

Like all true religious leaders, the Buddha taught that craving, possessiveness and envy are the cause of many personal and social ills; he preached against war and slavery, and denounced so-called holy practices that involved the sacrifice of human beings or animals. As a teacher he addressed himself to the rich and powerful, to the poor and weak. He disregarded class distinctions of the caste system and helped people whether they were high-born or scavengers; he admitted to his band of followers all those who chose to follow him. He reconciled quarrels between landowners and princes. He helped those who were distressed in mind or body to find a cure for their sickness. Here was no god or superhuman being; the Buddha did not rely on miracles or seek to divert the natural course of events. Rather he taught men to recognize the interdependence of cause and effect, to realize that in order to eradicate an undesired effect one must find out and eradicate the cause.

The Buddha advised that a state of peace could be attained and fully realized here, in this life, not by sacrifices to the gods, nor by prayers, but by ceaseless effort and by slowly perfected selflessness.

Buddhism is not a religion that one can accept blindly once and for all; it has to be understood and constantly questioned. The Buddha said 'Accept my words only after you have examined them for yourselves; do not accept them simply because of the reverence you have for me.'[1] Although in the course of time Buddhism has sometimes been affected by tradition, rituals, etc., its originator did not put it forward as anything more than a method to be experimented with. Self-reliance and tolerance are the keynotes of Buddhist thought. The Buddha said many times: 'You yourself must make the effort—Buddhas only point the way.'[2] Buddhism could never, therefore, be a proselytizing faith. Indeed the follower of the Buddha's teaching is exhorted to use that teaching only 'as a raft to cross the stream'. Once having attained the goal, Nibbāna, the raft must be abandoned.

The last words of the Buddha were these: 'Strive on heedfully'.[3]

[1] *Tattvasaṅgraha*, Vol. II, Gaekward Oriental Series, No. xxxi, 1926, v. 3588.
[2] Dh., v. 276.
[3] D., Vol. II, p. 156.

To abide in mindfulness is to see the world clearly and to see our fellow men clearly, without judgement, without envy, without hatred. To be able to do this we must know ourselves intimately and know the source of happiness and unhappiness within us.

II

Initiation into Buddhism

A unique feature in Buddhism is the omission of any ceremony akin to that of baptism. There is only one way to become a Buddhist and that is to follow in the footsteps of the Buddha and attempt to put his teaching into practice in one's life. Buddhist philosophy recognizes certain so-called 'fetters'[1] which hamper an individual's growth towards liberation. One of these fetters is 'the belief in rites and rituals', the mistaken assumption that by going through a special ceremony or by following some 'religious' practice, one can be saved. Little wonder then that there is no baptismal service in Buddhism. 'Work out your own liberation'[2] and never mind joining any groups or societies.

What, then, marks one's entry into Buddhism? The required quality is *saddhā*, often translated as 'faith', but meaning rather 'confidence based on knowledge'. As the Buddha said: 'Confidence is the companion to the person, and wisdom issues commands to him.'[3] Another interesting translation of *saddhā* is 'the confidence that there is a goal to be reached'. Before one can begin seriously to follow the Buddhist path, there must arise within one, however falteringly, the confidence that there is a path to be trodden and a goal to be reached. This initial confidence

---

[1] There are 10 fetters which bind one to rebirth (*dasa-saṃyojana*): (i) self-delusion (*sakkāyadiṭṭhi*), (ii) uncertainty (*vicikicchā*), (iii) belief or clinging to rites and rituals (*sīlabbataparāmāsa*), (iv) sensual lust (*kāmarāga*), (v) ill-will (*paṭigha*), (vi) greed for fine material existence (*rūparāga*), (vii) greed for immaterial existence (*arūparāga*), (viii) conceit (*māna*), (ix) restlessness (*uddhacca*), (x) ignorance (*avijjā*).

[2] Dh., v. 276: *Tumhehi kiccaṃ ātappaṃ.*

[3] S., I, pp. 25, 38.

may then be strengthened gradually, as experience teaches that it was well founded. Yet always, throughout one's long journey, this response of the heart, this awakening of confidence will precede, enabling one to take each new step in the dark.

It is no doubt in recognition of this repeated pattern—initial confidence leading to a willingness to experiment, which in turn brings confirmation of the original confidence and provides the basis from which a further step can be envisaged—that the Buddhist practice of *Tisaraṇa* was instituted and developed.

Tisaraṇa, 'the taking of the three refuges', involves the three-fold repetition of the following formula:

To the Buddha I go for refuge.
To the Dhamma (teaching) I go for refuge.
To the Sangha (order of monks) I go for refuge.

To the sceptical Westerner, such an incantation no doubt smacks of idolatry, superstition and 'oriental passiveness'. Yet taking refuge in the Buddha implies no personal guarantee that he him-self will effect the arrival at the goal of any of his followers. On the contrary he said: 'Surely by oneself is evil done, by oneself one becomes impure, by oneself evil is avoided, by oneself one becomes pure. Purity and impurity are (of the) individual. No one purifies another.'[1]

Indeed the *Tisaraṇa* would probably be more acceptable to the Western mind if, instead of the time-honoured 'refuge', the word *guide* were used. The first 'refuge' might then be translated as 'I intend to use the example of the Buddha to guide me in my search'.

The second guide is the *Dhamma*, the teaching. The example of the Buddha's own life is a great help to those wishing to attain a similar goal, just as the life of Christ affords a pattern to inspire and guide the sincere Christian; the Buddhist has a second guide in the detailed teaching handed down through the ages, just as

[1] Dh., v. 161.

the Christian has a similar guide in the sermons and parables of Christ recorded in the Gospels. The Buddhist is, however, yet more fortunate in that the Buddha lived for many years after his enlightenment and had the time to develop and perfect a detailed philosophy, a code of life, a careful step-by-step analysis of the path to be taken and the various states to be achieved and transcended. In the course of his teaching life the Buddha encountered many thousands of people, with differing educational, social, moral and religious backgrounds. He adapted and refined his message to suit the needs and the capabilities of kings and beggars, prostitutes and ascetics. The modern-day Buddhist can, therefore, turn confidently to the Teaching (*Dhamma*) for support, knowing that this teaching has been developed to incorporate all sorts and conditions of men. As he begins to put the teaching into practice, moreover, the follower of the Buddha comes to have a much surer and more intimate reason for relying on the *Dhamma:* he comes to realize that though he knows little— and practises less—he is beginning to be helped and 'succoured' by the teaching. He goes to the *Dhamma* for support because he begins to find that its message is in accord with his own slowly, and probably painfully, acquired experience.

The third refuge is the *Sangha*, the community of monks, past, present and future. The realization that millions of men have followed the Buddha's teaching, have decided to devote their whole energy and attention to it, and have found it a valid and satisfying way of life—this is the third guide for the Buddhist. *Sangha* can be interpreted as the community or order of monks, but it can also be interpreted as the fellowship of those who have walked in the footsteps of the Buddha and reaped the fruit of their labours.

III

The Negative Aspects of
Buddhist Morality

When through reading, hearing and pondering the teaching, one has established some basic confidence in it, the first steps on the path can be taken. In Buddhism, as in most other religions, these first steps involve an examination of the code of morality by which one's life in the world is governed. Before turning to the inner life, to the development and liberation of the mind—which is the goal of Buddhist teaching—the outer life has to be put in order. Yet here again all is not as simple as it seems, and Buddhist morality cannot be thought of as just another set of rules. In making a choice, there must be cultivation of wisdom and discernment to detect when a choice should be made. Of cultivation of will-power and cultivation of discernment the Buddhist teaching stresses the latter more than the former, for blind obedience is not encouraged, and so unless a person is convinced that he is pursuing an unwise course he is unlikely to abandon it if it is attractive to him.

Buddhist morality is, in fact, a natural morality; it is based on an individual's understanding, through experience, of the results of his actions, and on his own conscious informed choice to follow this way rather than that. No external agent is invoked; one is not asked to obey the commandments of God; neither fear nor love are involved, only understanding based on experiment and careful choice.

This approach is exemplified in the formula used by Buddhists to set forth their code of morality. Here is no law, no 'thou shalt' or 'thou shalt not'. The Buddhist is invited to 'take upon himself' certain 'rules of training', which he may find helpful in achieving that quiet self-reliance indispensable to the seeker after harmony and happiness. There is no lawgiver, there are no commandments, but there is an appeal to commonsense and to social order.

The moral foundation on which the Buddha's teaching is built is formulated as the 'five precepts':

1. I undertake the rule of training to refrain from harming living things.
2. I undertake the rule of training to refrain from taking what is not given.
3. I undertake the rule of training to refrain from a misuse of the senses.
4. I undertake the rule of training to refrain from wrong speech.
5. I undertake the rule of training to refrain from taking drugs or drinks which tend to cloud the mind.

The first precept implies a growing awareness of the sanctity of life. Often translated as 'not to kill', this precept requires rather that one cease to abuse, injure or in any way harm living things. At first it may seem that to abstain from murder or wanton killing is all that is meant. Then gradually the 'rule of training' begins to take on a new significance. The question arises whether my gastronomical pleasure should be satisfied at the expense of 'living things', whether animals should be slaughtered so that I may disport myself in their borrowed plumes. And then the questions begin to go deeper. What of my murderous impulses when I am thwarted or humiliated? What of the secret joy I feel when someone I dislike is 'put down'?

If a man living in the Western world in the mid-twentieth century tries seriously to put into practice the first precept of the Buddhist moral code, an ever-increasing number of questions and doubts will arise in him. Yet such questions are fruitful. At first, of course, they disturb and disrupt his life, but gradually, as they are faced and worked through, life itself acquires a new significance and a new perspective. A new sense of respect—

for oneself and for others—begins to permeate one's thinking.

The second precept requires one to abstain from 'taking what is not given'. Here again the easy interpretation—'Do not steal' —is blatantly inadequate. Rather it is a question of developing towards the owners of inanimate objects that same respect that the first precept enjoins towards living things.

'Not taking what is not given' necessitates waiting until things are offered rather than rushing out and grabbing them. A quiet, reflective patience will gradually replace the frantic 'I want' attitude so prevalent today. But, as in the case of the first precept, a sincere attempt to put into practice the 'rule of training to refrain from taking what is not given' will involve us in much deep self-questioning.

The third precept has been frequently translated as 'abstaining from sexual misconduct'. Yet this is not the complete story. What we are here advised to refrain from is the misuse of the body and the bodily sensations. Artificial stimulation of the appetite for food is involved as much as is adultery or incest. He who undertakes this third rule of training is required to reflect on the way in which he uses his body, the way in which he uses his sense organs and his sexual drives.

This is not an appeal for asceticism. The Buddhist is not asked to abstain from sex; he is not asked to abstain from eating the food that pleases him nor from feasting his eyes or ears on such works of art or of nature as attract him. What the third rule of training advocates is a ceaseless awareness of the quality and degree of one's sensual activity. The senses are to be enjoyed but not jaded, to be used but not abused. It is not marriage that makes sex permissible but mutual respect and trust. It is not luxury in itself that is to be shunned, but the swamping of consciousness by excessive indulgence of any kind and the avoidance of causing suffering to others.

There are many lists, in Buddhist canonical literature, of the varieties of 'wrong speech'. Lying is, of course, one variety, so is slander, back-biting, gossip, malicious talk, talk designed to stir up hatred or violence in the listeners, repetition of secrets told in confidence and so on.

The implications for the modern Buddhist of the terms 'right speech' and 'wrong speech' will be dealt with at greater length later in the discussion of the third factor of the eightfold path (see p. 49).

For the moment it may suffice to note that a careful attempt to put into practice the fourth precept will necessarily involve one in a ceaseless search for self honesty.

From the psychotic—who believes that he is Napoleon, and whose assertion to this effect will withstand a lie-detector test—to the 'normal' person—who conveniently 'forgets' pieces of information that would contradict his presentation of a case—the progression is complex but unbroken. To observe conscientiously the fourth rule of training leads us to question how it is we 'forget' some things, how it is we say things 'we didn't mean' why it is people sometimes misinterpret what we say. Is it due to our own lack of clarity, or is it simply their failure to comprehend? It leads us to watch more closely whether extra trimmings get added to a tale when we retell it. We begin to reflect on the things we say to people, and instead of pouring out our story to whomsoever happens to be around, we pause to consider what effects this may have on them, and whether any harm is likely to come —to them or to us—from the telling.

To avoid wrong speech is not an easy task, and few could claim to have succeeded in it fully. Yet however imperfectly we observe it we can notice the difference when we undertake this fourth precept. Here again we find that life becomes gentler and quieter, as the speed and the noise begin to abate. Speaking perhaps a little less, we find that we have time to listen a little more—a rare virtue in the modern world.

The fifth precept contains a clue to the interpretation of the entire code of Buddhist morality: 'I undertake the rule of training to refrain from drugs and drinks which tend to cloud the mind.' As what is harmful, according to the Buddhist concept of human ethics, is the deliberate clouding of the mind.

The central teaching of the Buddha is a system of meditation designed so to clarify the mind that knowledge and insight may arise therein and be reflected without impediment. As an essential preparation, therefore, the would-be follower of this teaching undertakes to train himself to refrain from indulgence in any drink or drug that would tend to impair the clarity of his mental vision, that would tend to smother his doubts and uncertainties in a cloud of semi-conscious euphoria, or that would encourage him to see things as other than they really are.

IV
The Positive Aspects of Buddhist Morality

The Buddha's teaching has been described in three short axioms:

Cease to do evil;
Learn to do good;
Purify your own mind.[1]

The first line sums up the code of morality contained in the five precepts. This is, however, only a clearing away of the weeds from the soil, and the constructive work begins with the second line: learn to do good.

Scattered throughout Buddhist literature are various lists of 'wholesome' states, or 'things to be encouraged', and these are contrasted with the 'unwholesome' states, or things to be discouraged. One of the most prominent of the 'wholesome' states is *dāna*—meaning 'giving'.

Over the centuries *dāna* has come to have a rather narrow, restricted and materialistic meaning—with the *caritas* principle of the New Testament. But if we look at the early descriptions and illustrations of *dāna* we find that this was not the original intention.

What is to be encouraged is not the habit of giving to charitable institutions from time to time, not a mechanical payment of the tithe, not, to put it bluntly, the practice of buying an easy conscience at the cheapest rate. *Dāna* implies gradually developing the will to give—whenever and however the need arises.

Western readers would probably best understand the spirit of

[1] Dh., v. 183.

the Buddhist virtue of *dāna* if he were to turn back to reconsider the description of *caritas* in the epistle to the Corinthians:

'And though I distribute all my goods (to the poor), and offer my body to be burned (as a sacrifice), yet it will profit me nothing unless I have love. Love is long-suffering and kind; love is not jealous, nor does it vaunt itself . . . love does not reckon the wrong that has been done to it, nor is it easily provoked.'[1]

Here we are brought into the area of another Buddhist virtue: *mettā*. *Dāna* is one outward manifestation of concern for the welfare of others, *mettā* (often translated as loving-kindness) embraces the whole sphere of that concern. To develop *mettā* is to develop the state of mind wherein the joys and sorrows, the well-being and the problems of others are as important to me as are my own. *Mettā* requires the breaking down of the barriers in one's thinking between oneself and the rest of humanity. It has often been said that the follower of the Buddha should endeavour to feel towards all men—relations, friends, acquaintances and enemies—just as a mother feels towards her child. A difficult task, no doubt, but one which, according to the Buddhist code, is desirable before much progress in spiritual development is possible.

Another indispensable virtue, allied to *mettā* and yet perhaps a little more difficult for the non-Buddhist to understand, is the 'transference of merit'. St Paul says of love that it 'seeketh not its own things'.[2] The Buddhist virtue of transference of merit might be considered as a development of this theme. 'Cease to do evil; learn to do good' it has been said; yet a time comes when one must realize that there is selfishness inherent in one's abstinence from evil and one's pursuit of good. 'It becomes apparent to me that I am doing good in order that I may reap the benefits—

[1] *Corinthians*, I, 13, III–V.
[2] *Ibid.*, xiii, v. 5.

whether they be in the form of increased respect from others, or merely increased self-respect. I am working and striving in order that I may go to heaven—whether that heaven be an after-death world peopled by angels playing harps, or whether it be a state of well-being and self-satisfaction in this life.' It is at this point that the practice of the 'transference of merit' is to be developed. The Buddhist learns to will that the benefits of his good actions return not to him alone but to all men. Each act of generosity, each movement of love, is no longer to be totted up in my personal account book but is to rebound to the benefit of all. Rather like a stream which feeds the ocean and which is replenished, not by means of the same water flowing back to it, but in the course of time with the falling of the rains.

The practice of transference of merit is a difficult one, the pitfalls are many and subtly disguised, yet it is a concept to which many of us might give much closer consideration.

Finally, in this brief and necessarily superficial survey of Buddhist 'wholesome 'practices, we might consider the virtue of 'rejoicing in other people's merit'. That such a virtue is difficult to attain may be inferred from reading the admonitions of St Teresa of Avila and of the author of *The Cloud of Unknowing*. 'Rejoicing in other people's merit' cannot be experienced until a considerable amount of loving-kindness (*mettā*) has been developed, and until some attempt has been made to understand the concept of the 'transference of merit'. Rejoicing in someone else's merit can be infinitely more difficult than rejoicing in the promotion of someone else to the appointment you wanted. Here again the virtue is not to be cultivated for its own sake—because the Buddha said you should. Rejoicing in other people's merit, in their moral excellence and in their spiritual growth, is one of the methods suggested which the follower of the Buddha may find useful in breaking down the artificial barriers which he has erected between one individual and another.

Part Two
Philosophy

V

The First Noble Truth

Including a Discussion of Impermanence (*Anicca*)

Buddhism not being a revealed religion, at least not in the usual sense of the word, is based wholly on human experience. The follower of the Buddha is exhorted to believe nothing until he has experienced it and found it to be true.

We shall consider now, in the second part of this book, the main tenets of Buddhist philosophy. It must at all times be remembered, however, that these 'truths' are not presented to the would-be Buddhist as articles of faith in which he must believe in order to be saved. They are the result of one man's search for truth and freedom, and they have been found valid by many millions who followed after him; but each individual, in so far as he is a true follower of the Buddha, must reason out each step for himself, and must in time come to experience the truth, not by hearsay but by direct knowledge during his own lifetime. Until that day of his own enlightenment, he will not be able to appreciate fully the profundity and sublimity of the Buddha's teaching.

The first truth to which the Buddha awakened on the night of the full moon of May was the truth of suffering (*dukkha*).

The most placid and happy-natured among us would admit that many things in this life are *dukkha*. There is physical and mental sickness, there is pain. There is the grief and sorrow occasioned by the loss of, or separation from, that which one loves. There is death:

'Not in the sky, nor in mid-ocean, nor in entering a mountain cave, is found that place on earth where abiding one will not be overcome by death.'[1]

[1] Dh., v. 128.

Those of a less contented nature might add to this list the frustration that results from not getting what one wants, or from being tied to what one hates. Who of us have not experienced the suffering attendant upon anger, who has never known fear, loneliness and despair?

Long before chemistry and physics discovered the transience and instability of matter/energy, the Buddha had 'realized' the fundamental impermanence of all phenomena—including everything that a man can call his 'self'; body and mind, sensations, perceptions and feelings are impermanent and subject to change. And since they are impermanent, they are unsatisfactory, they are *dukkha*. Two thousand five hundred years before the Existential *angst* shattered the complacency of industrial Europe, Buddhist monks sat in meditation and were silently shattered by the same anguish as the knowledge arose within them that all things are in a state of flux, and that suffering is built into the very structure of existence.

The realization that existence itself is suffering, that pleasure is but 'gilded pain', and that death is the only certainty—this realization has led many men into many different paths. For some the experience has been so catastrophic that only suicide or madness could release them from the memory of it. For others there has been a less dramatic but equally tragic flight into the realms of the *acte gratuit* or of *l'humour noir*. Others have turned to drugs, to drink, to perversions or diversions of one kind and another. Some have become power maniacs, some tramps. Some have taken to gambling, others have 'seen the light and been saved'. The Buddha went on into the centre of the knowledge of the truth of suffering, and penetrated its cause. And this is what Buddhists call the 'second noble truth': the truth of the cause of suffering.

VI
The Second Noble Truth
(Including a Discussion of
Paṭiccasamuppāda and Rebirth) ✓

If we are to understand, even in a rudimentary fashion, the truth of the cause of suffering, we must touch upon and attempt to unravel some of the most complex and subtle aspects of the Buddha's teaching. We shall have to consider, for example, the 'chain of dependent origination' and the doctrine of rebirth.

Starting with the experiential fact of the transient and unsatisfactory nature of human existence, the Buddha set out to discover the implications of that impermanence and the cause of that unease. He found that the two threads were intertwined and interdependent. It is through failure to realize the truth of impermannence, through grasping at the 'constant flux' as though it were something stable, that man is caught up in the whirlpool of suffering.

The chain of interdependent links that binds men to the wheel of suffering is called *Paṭiccasamuppāda*. This is a cycle of causation; Buddhism posits no first cause but a series of interconnected links in a (vicious) circle from which there is no apparent escape.

The doctrine of *paṭiccasamuppāda* (dependent origination) is one of the most subtle teachings in the scriptures of the world; the Buddha himself claimed:

'Profound indeed is this teaching of *paṭiccasamuppāda*. . . . It is through not understanding and penetrating this doctrine that beings have become entangled like a matted ball of thread.'[1]

To penetrate the doctrine of *paṭiccasamuppāda* is to penetrate to
[1] D., II, p. 55; S., II, p. 92, iv, p. 158.

the very core of existence. All we shall attempt to do here is to present an outline of the teaching in as simple terms as possible. As we grow older, more experienced and, we hope, wiser, new depths of the teaching and new possibilities of interpretation will become apparent.

The twelve links of *paṭiccasamuppāda* apply, whether we are considering a single moment of time or a whole lifetime. It will probably be less confusing for the Western reader if we present here a possible interpretation of this doctrine as it operates within a stretch of time neither as short as a moment nor as long as a lifetime. It must be stressed that this is only one suggested interpretation of *paṭiccasamuppāda*. At the end of the book the English terms for the twelve links are given. The only way we can hope to understand this 'subtle *paṭiccasamuppāda*' is by pondering on it constantly and conscientiously until we begin to comprehend its labyrinthine ways. At times it will seem very clear to us, and beautifully logical; then again our vision will be temporarily clouded over as we begin to penetrate to another layer of meaning.

The first-named link in the chain is ignorance—the failure to realize the truth, the lack of insight into the reality of things. In this soil of delusion subconscious impulses or drives arise. Because of our basic ignorance, these drives are not recognized for what they are—impermanent and illusory—but are allowed to flourish and bear fruit. Finally, though still unrecognized, they erupt into the conscious mind. Consciousness, as unenlightened as the sub-conscious drives from which it arose, immediately begins to classify and arrange. Instead of the 'constant flux', consciousness posits a stable world of identifiable things. This world of 'ten thousand things' impinges on our senses, and forthwith an emotional reaction is produced. We find the experience pleasant or unpleasant or we 'couldn't care less' and sink back into sleep. This emotional reaction creates a craving; if the experience is pleasant we seek it out, if unpleasant we recoil from it. Out of this craving arises clinging as we lapse into the habit of grabbing or of rejecting. Our response is no longer attuned to the stimulus, which may in fact have ceased to please or displease us, but we continue to cling to it because it is familiar. In this way we are led on towards a new situation but still encumbered with the attitudes of the past. The new situation arises, comes to maturity, decays and passes away. We are back where we started. The experience has taught us nothing. All it has done for us is to add another thread to the rope that binds us to the wheel of suffering.

This terrifying prospect—worthy of the imaginative art of the middle ages—of man, blind and naked, spinning on a wheel of torment, might well prompt us to jump off the wheel by means of suicide. But here we are checked abruptly by the doctrine of rebirth. Suicide will not enable us to jump off the wheel; we are tied to it beyond death.

During the night of his enlightenment the Buddha experienced two aspects of rebirth. He reviewed his own previous lives and he witnessed the arising and passing away of others. The doctrine of dependent origination itself is usually taught, at least in the East, as a description of the process whereby one life is linked to the next. We must be careful here to distinguish between transmigration and rebirth. Transmigration posits a soul that migrates from one life to another. Rebirth does not speak of a soul nor of any 'thing' passing over.

During one lifetime we fondly imagine that we and our world are stable. Despite the obvious examples of change and decay, of erratic feelings and unpredictable moods, despite the process of growth and decline, despite the microscopic experiments of scientists, we continue to behave as though we were something permanent, something identifiable and 'real'. The Buddha's answer to this attitude was to ask: Where is the 'I'? Is it the body? Is it the feelings? Is it the will? or the mind? Nowhere can be found a permanent identity. What then 'passes over' after death?

The reply is simple yet unexpected. Life is a constant flux. What we recognize as one lifetime is merely a specific manifestation of this flux. At death the pattern is disturbed but the flux continues. If we try to jump off the wheel by committing suicide we merely interrupt one manifestation of flux. In so far as 'we' existed before, we continue to exist.

The various schools of Buddhism have elaborated different explanations of the way in which the patterns, established during one lifetime, are interrupted at death, reform and re-establish themselves. It may be that the moment of death is followed immediately by the rebirth moment. It may be that there is an intervening period during which the patterns have time to re-cluster themselves and form new combinations. But just as we cannot destroy the energy mass that we call our body—though we crush it, burn it or blow it to pieces—so we cannot destroy the other aspects of 'our' life: mind with its feelings, sensations, etc. The flux continues, the chain of dependent origination remains unbroken, the cause of suffering persists—whether we will or not.

The second noble truth is the truth of the cause of suffering. Briefly that cause is craving: craving for sensual satisfaction, craving for existence, craving for non-existence. Freud was remarkably close to Buddhist classifications when he defined the basic human drives as libido and morbido. Conjoined with craving is delusion. These two root-causes breed the illusion of possession: this is my house, my reputation, my life. We grasp at an illusion and run chasing after it 'down the days and down the nights', dreaming and waking, from one life to the next.

VII
The Third Noble Truth
(Including a Discussion of *Anattā*)

The Buddha said: I teach but two things—*dukkha* and the release from *dukkha*.[1] The third noble truth is the truth of the cessation of *dukkha*. It has been said that if you hurl a stick and hit a dog, a dog will snarl at the stick and attack it; if you hurl a stick at a lion, the lion will ignore the stick and attack you. A similar comparison was drawn by the Buddha between the teachings of others and his own teaching; other religions have attacked the symptoms, spreading a salve of one kind or another on the raw wound of human suffering; the teaching of the Buddha, on the other hand, maintains that only by the eradication of the cause of *dukkha* can a state be reached in which *dukkha*, no longer arises.

This state, the state of the non-arising of *dukkha*, is called *Nibbāna*.

Nibbāna defies description in the same way as does 'the kingdom of heaven' of the *Gospel according to St Thomas*. It has been called the deathless, the other shore. Being uncompounded, it is not subject to the three characteristics of all compounded things: impermanence, *dukkha* and substancelessness. It is compared to the wind. '*Nibbāna* is uncompounded; it is made of nothing at all. One cannot say of *Nibbāna* that it arises or that it does not arise, or that it is to be produced, or that it is past or future or present, or that it is cognizable by the eye, ear, nose, tongue or body.' It is, however, cognizable by the mind.

There are two extremes which one must avoid in trying to understand the concept of *Nibbāna*. Firstly, one must avoid

[1] M., I, p. 140.

comparing *Nibbāna* with any kind of personal god. The doctrine of no-self, which we mentioned in the previous chapter in connection with an individual human life, applies too in connection with *Nibbāna*. Even the uncompounded, the deathless *Nibbāna* is *anattā*—without a self. *Nibbāna*, though not bound by the phenomenal world of suffering, is not separate from it. The other pitfall to be avoided is to identify the attainment of *Nibbāna* with annihilation. Here we should refer the reader to the discussion on suicide (p. 41); just as there is no 'self' that can jump off the wheel, so there is no self that can be annihilated by the attainment of *Nibbāna*. *Nibbāna* is the non-arising of all conditioned states; there will no longer be any 'being' swept away on the round of suffering.

The fourth noble truth outlines the practical means by which *Nibbāna* is to be realized; but before announcing it the Buddha cleared away certain misconceptions which were current at the time and which had proved a serious hindrance in the quest for truth. In the first discourse after his Enlightenment, delivered to the five disciples who had deserted him when he abandoned the path of self-mortification, he explained that there are two extreme courses to be avoided; on the one hand that of excessive sensual indulgence, which is unprofitable and ignoble, and on the other the practice of extreme physical asceticism, which is painful, impure, vain and unprofitable.

In contrast to these stands 'The Middle Path' which the Buddha discovered; the Path which enables one to see and to know, which leads to peace, to discernment, to full knowledge, to *Nibbāna*.

VIII
The Fourth Noble Truth
(Including a Discussion of *Kamma/Vipāka*)

The fourth noble truth is the truth of the way leading to the cessation of suffering; it is a map of the path to *Nibbāna*. It has been said of *Nibbāna* that it is causeless, that it is not born of *kamma*,[1] but the way leading to the realization of Nibbana is subject to the law of cause and effect.

Here we must digress a little to discuss some of the salient points of the Buddhist doctrine of *kamma/vipāka*—the interdependence of cause and effect.

The Buddhist path to liberation is built on the universal law—which to the Buddha and to many who came after him, was an experienced fact—of the interdependence of cause and effect. Nothing, according to the Buddhist view, arises without a cause. The doctrine of *kamma/vipāka* cuts firmly across the controversy between fatalism and free will. We are conditioned by all that we have been, by all that has been said, thought or done in countless previous lives; yet in this present moment we are, consciously or unconsciously, determining the future. Our life now, at this very moment, is both the *vipāka* of the past and the *kamma* of the future. The *kamma/vipāka* law explains why Buddhism is often referred to as the teaching of the here and now. For here and

---

[1] *Kamma*, in Pali, and *karma*, in Sanskrit, in its most general sense means all good and bad actions. *Kamma* is neither fatalism nor a doctrine of predetermination. The past influences the present, for *kamma* is past as well as present. The past and present influence the future—in this life or in the life to come. The Buddha has said: 'It is mental volition, O monks, that I call *kamma*. Having willed, one acts through body, speech or mind.' (A., III, p. 415.)

now is the only sphere in which man can influence—and may eventually interrupt—the chain of *kamma/vipāka*.

The intricate interplay of the myriad strands of *kamma/vipāka*, some reinforcing each other, some counterbalancing, some fading, some waxing strong, is said to have been one of the meditational experiences which arose in the mind of the Buddha during the night of his Enlightenment.

In Buddhist terminology all thought, action and speech is said to be rooted in one of two types of consciousness—*kusala* or *akusala*, wholesome or unwholesome. If the root is generosity, compassion or insight, the resultant act constitutes wholesome *kamma* and will produce correspondingly beneficial effects. If the root is greed, hatred or delusion, unwholesome *kammic* acts result, leading to undesirable effects. The initial function of the 'way leading to the cessation of suffering' is to help one to eliminate unwholesomely rooted *kamma* and begin to cultivate those states of mind which will bring only beneficial results. It has been frequently pointed out, however, that one cannot in this teaching expect quick returns; although our present actions may be reasonably, even uncomfortably, 'wholesome', we may find ourselves overwhelmed by misfortunes and distress; this does not disprove the law of *kamma/vipāka*, however, nor is it an excuse for returning to our old comfortable rut. Our present distress is but the effect (*vipāka*) of the past, and in order to forestall its recurrence in the future we need to consider what crop we are now sowing.

The path leading to the release from suffering is said to be eight-fold. These are not consecutive steps. The eight factors are interdependent and must be perfected simultaneously, the fulfilment of one factor being unlikely without at least the partial development of the others. These eight factors are:

1. *sammā diṭṭhi*   right understanding or views
2. *sammā saṅkappa*   right thought or motives
2. *sammā vācā*   right speech

4. *sammā kammanta*   right action
5. *sammā ājīva*   right means of livelihood
6. *sammā vāyāma*   right effort
7. *sammā sati*   right mindfulness
8. *sammā samādhi*   right concentration.

It is important to realize that the word *sammā* prefixing each of the eight factors has a wide range of meaning. In this context it can mean right as opposed to wrong, or it can, in the developed follower of the path, come to mean completed or perfected.

The initial task of one wishing to follow the eight-fold path is to observe oneself carefully and see which factors have already been developed to a certain extent and which are still in a very rudimentary condition. (Some people, for example, have developed their thinking faculty but their ability to communicate with other people is almost non-existent. Others, on the contrary, find it easy to form relationships but have an undeveloped reflective faculty.) The weak aspects of character or of life will then have to be brought into balance and harmony with the strong.

We shall proceed now to consider each factor of the path in turn. Our method will be similar to that employed in connection with the doctrine of *paṭiccasamuppāda*, and a similar warning must be given. The interpretations here are suggestions only. As with every other philosophical 'truth', the truth of the way to the cessation of suffering will have little meaning or relevance if it is studied coldly and objectively; but as each factor is quietly reviewed and gradually assimilated into daily life, some of its value and depth will begin to be appreciated.

1. *Sammā diṭṭhi* (right understanding or views) in the initial stages of one's practice of the path need mean little more than a vague recognition that 'all is not what it seems'. Right understanding implies in the first instance having seen through the delusion that material security automatically brings peace of mind, or that ceremonies and ritual can wipe out the effects of a past act. Gradually, as the path is perfected, right views, based on

knowledge, replace the previous delusions or superstitions that were based on ignorance and lack of insight.

The first factor of the path is then concerned with the contents of the mind. In order to develop this factor one must cease to think mechanically, and begin to question one's previous assumptions, until all erroneous views have been replaced by views based on an understanding of things as they really are.

One must see life as it is, in accordance with its three characteristics of impermanence (*anicca*), dissatisfactoriness (*dukkha*) and egolessness (*anattā*); one must possess a clear understanding of the nature of existence, of the moral law, of the factors and component elements that go to make up *saṃsāra*. In short, one must have a clear understanding of *paṭiccasamuppāda* and the Four Noble Truths. On the basis of understanding these facts one can perceive the causes of the vicissitudes of life.

2. *Sammā saṅkappa*, usually translated as right thought or right motives, seems to apply to the emotional basis of thought rather than to thinking itself. As the first factor of the path is concerned with the content and direction of thought, the second factor is concerned with the quality of the drive behind the thinking.

It is quite possible, and even at present quite fashionable, to hold opinions that would be called by a Buddhist 'right views', and yet the emotional drive behind those views may not be 'right' at all. It is possible, for example, to be driven by an unrecognized fear of involvement to adopt the view that 'all is impermanent'. Similarly a pathological inability to relax or to enjoy oneself can lead one to grasp at the view that 'all is suffering' —the fault being thereby shifted from within to without. The doctrine that there is no permanent, abiding soul or personal identity can easily find favour with one who has never succeeded in forming a satisfactory relationship with another—or with himself. The development of 'right thought' implies gradually uncovering and resolving these unrecognized drives. It implies weeding out the 'unwholesome' roots and encouraging the 'wholesome' roots of generosity and unselfishness, kindness and compassion, wisdom and insight.

Sammā saṅkappa (right thought or motives) is that quality of consciousness wherein there is no obstruction to the thought processes. Sometimes, although to an observer one may seem to be reasoning logically and clearly, one is dimly aware of an emotional block that is in fact controlling the direction of one's reasoning and preventing it from penetrating beyond a certain point. *Sammā saṅkappa* is the absence of all such emotional obstructions. It denotes a state of consciousness that is limpid, clear, cool, free from the limiting considerations of self-interest, without tension or veiled uneasiness.

This means that one's mind should be pure, free from carnal 'thirst' (*rāga*), malevolence (*vyāpāda*), cruelty (*vihiṃsā*) and the like. At the same time, one should be willing to relinquish anything that obstructs one's onward march.

3. *Sammā vācā* (right speech). By not indulging in, or listening to, lying, back-biting, harsh talk and idle gossip, we can establish a connecting link between 'right thought' and 'right action'. *Sammā vācā* is free from dogmatic assertions and from hypnotic suggestions; it is an instrument whereby one can learn and teach, comfort and be comforted. We are practising right speech when we use conversation as a means of coming to know people, to understand them and ourselves. This last sentence may seem a little ridiculous if looked at superficially: What else, one might ask, could conversation be used for? Yet one has only to sit in a bus or train and listen to the 'conversations' going on around to realize that they are very rarely examples of right speech. Most so-called conversations are a series of interrupted monologues: each member of the group speaks more or less in order, but no one listens or makes any attempt to respond.

The practice of this third factor of the path implies a gradual but radical change in our use of language. At the time the eightfold path was expounded the spoken word was the main medium of communication; but what is here set down as 'right speech' should now be interpreted as 'right communication'—whether that take the form of radio or TV programmes, advertising material, newspapers, magazines or books. The development of *sammā vācā* should lead to a gradual refining of our use of all forms of communication. We shall come to realize the destructive nature of hypnotic TV advertisements, sensational newspaper articles and escapist literature of all kinds. We shall come to realize the dangers as well as the immense potential value of conversation.

Right speech, then, means using the various modes of communication to further our search for understanding and insight.

It would not only be characterized by wisdom but also by kindness. Right speech should not be unduly excitable, not prompted by infatuation or selfish interests. It should not be such as to inflame the passions.

The person of right speech has been explained by the Buddha as follows:

'He avoids lying. He speaks the truth. Wherever he may be he never knowingly speaks a lie, either for the sake of his own advantage, or for the sake of another person's advantage, or for the sake of any advantage whatsoever. He avoids tale bearing. What he has heard here, he does not repeat there, so as to cause dissension there; and what he has heard there, he does not repeat here, so as to cause dissension here. Thus he unites those that are divided; and those that are united, he encourages. Concord gladdens him, he delights and rejoices in concord; and it is concord that he spreads by his words. He avoids harsh language. He speaks such words as are gentle, soothing to the ear, loving, such words as go to the heart, and are courteous and friendly, and agreeable to many. He avoids vain talk. He speaks at the right time, in accordance with facts, speaks what is useful, speaks of the law and the discipline; his speech is like a treasure, uttered at the right moment, accompanied by arguments, moderate and full of sense.'[1]

'He uses such speech which is harmless, pleasant to the ear, agreeable, touching the heart, courteous, delightful to many and pleasant to many. This one is called "the honey-tongued"'.[2]

4. *Sammā kammanta* (right action). This involves much more than just keeping the precepts (see pp. 28–30). In the early stages of the practice of the path, keeping the precepts will probably require such an effort that there will be little energy left for any more advanced development of right action. Gradually, however, as the unwholesome patterns are weakened and we begin to build up some positive virtues (see pp. 32–4), the further implications of *sammā kammanta* can be considered.

Right action is any action that proceeds from an unobstructed mind. Whereas morality, in the usual sense of the word, can be practised by one who is blind to the motives behind this behaviour right action is impossible without a clear and deep understanding.

The *path* of right action involves abstaining from unwholesome *kamma* and performing only those actions which will lead to beneficial results. The *goal* of right action, however, is to transcend even *kusala* (wholesome) *kamma*, for once the enlightenment experience has arisen in life, actions will cease to produce any *kammic* results, harmful or beneficial. The *Upanishads* put it slightly differently: 'Only actions done in God bind not the soul of man',[3] but the meaning is similar. Although for many years and perhaps for many lifetimes we shall have to strive to develop the fourth factor in the sense of 'wholesome practices', when once the path has been fully perfected, actions will no longer have any binding effect, will no longer form part of the *kamma/vipāka* chain.

5. *Sammā ājīva* (right means of livelihood). The simplest interpretation of this factor of the path is based on the five pre-

[1] A., v, p. 264 f.   [2] *Ibid.*, I, p. 128.
[3] Īsopaniṣad, v. 2.

cepts. Conscientious observance of the five precepts automatically vetos certain trades and professions. The first precept—not to harm living things—requires that we do not earn our living by means of butchering cattle, dealing in flesh, fishing, hunting and so forth. Neither may one make or use weapons, nor engage in any form of warfare. Similarly the fifth precept—not to indulge in drinks or drugs that tend to cloud the mind—prevents us not only from trafficking in drugs, but also from engaging in the manufacture or distribution of alcohol. This straightforward interpretation of *sammā ājīva* makes a very useful beginning, but it is only a beginning. As soon as we delve a little deeper into the concept of right livelihood, a host of problems and further shades of meaning becomes apparent.

We shall list a few of the problems, without attempting to give any answers. The reader, if he tries to practise this factor of the path, will evolve his own answers—and, of course, an infinite number of further questions. Among the problems raised by an attempt to practice *sammā ājīva* are:

1. whether one can support, by working, paying taxes and accepting benefits, a government which is engaged in warfare, or actively preparing for it;
2. whether, in the name of the relief of human suffering, one can engage in medical research that involves sacrificing the lives of countless animals; and, more subtly, whether one can prescribe, sell—or even use—those drugs which have been discovered and tested by means of such experiments;
3. whether one has the right to destroy disease-bearing insects, or work in the preparation of materials for that purpose;
4. whether the third and fourth precepts would prohibit one from working in advertising or mass production work.

The list is endless. The questions are all ones that can only be answered by careful analysis of the circumstances, the motives and the attitudes of the people involved.

Even if one manages more or less to avoid the wrong means of livelihood, the problems are not yet over. *Sammā ājīva* implies much more than the mere avoiding of wrong means of livelihood. It implies a careful weighing up of our attributes and potentialities, and the selecting of a job that will use the talents we have and at the same time help to develop our weak points.

Briefly, then, we might say that the fifth factor of the path requires us to stop and consider how and why we are spending our working hours. It requires us to take time to think out and find some means of occupation which will be conducive to our own growth and development and which will, if possible, be beneficial to others. If a job helps us in our search for an understanding both of ourselves and of the world around us then it is, for us, *sammā ājīva*—no matter how futile and crazy it may seem to our friends and neighbours.

6. *Sammā vāyāma* (right effort). Although the canonical division of right effort into four categories seems at first sight to be rather pedantic and meaningless it has, if one studies it more closely, a sound practical and psychological validity. The four-fold division of right effort consists of:

1. the effort to cut off unwholesome states that have already arisen;
2. the effort to prevent the arising of unwholesome states that have not yet arisen;
3. the effort to preserve wholesome states that have already arisen;
4. the effort to encourage wholesome states that have not yet arisen.

Right effort requires the development of insight, intuition and will power. We need to develop insight in order to perceive which of the states of mind habitually present are to be preserved and which are to be weeded out. We need to develop intuition so that we can gauge when we are sailing close to a hitherto unknown state of mind and whether we should go ahead or withdraw from it.

This sixth factor, though dependent on insight and intuition, is primarily concerned with the development of the will. We mentioned earlier (p. 27) that Buddhism insists on the development of wisdom rather than of will power; nevertheless it recognizes the need for the latter and provides scope for the perfecting of it in this factor of the path. Without the constant and deliberate practice of right effort, no sure progress can be made.

7. *Sammā sati* (right mindfulness) is the pivotal factor of the path. Without it none of the other factors can be brought to completion. Right mindfulness serves too as a control over the other factors, preventing the excessive development of one at the expense of the others. In Christian terminology *sammā sati* might be translated as 'the practice of the presence of God'; it implies gradually extending one's awareness until every action, thought and word is performed in the full light of consciousness.

The practice of mindfulness has been described under four headings known as the four foundations of mindfulness, *sati-paṭṭhāna*. Firstly, mindfulness of the body: this consists in becoming gradually more aware of the body. We can begin this practice by trying to watch the various changes in the postures of the body—lying, sitting, standing, walking. Care must be taken to be neither too objective nor too subjective; we are not being asked to look at our bodies as 'things' moving puppet-like before the watching mind; nor are we asked to 'feel' very acutely every movement and gesture. What is required rather is that we try to live here and now 'in our bodies'. This may seem a bizarre request, but once we try to experience this state we realize how rarely in fact we are 'living in our bodies', how rarely we are aware of the movements of our limbs and the interplay of muscles. Mindfulness of the body can be practised too by watching the breath flowing in and out of the nostrils, by listening to sounds impinging on the ear, not pausing to name and pass judgement on them, but just noting their arising and passing away. We can learn to become aware of the taste and texture of food, not after the manner of the gourmet or the connoisseur, not for the sake of becoming an expert in the detection of spices or in the selection of wines, but simply in order to intensify our awareness, noting the order and intensity of sensations, the variety of flavours, temperatures, colours, etc.

For some, and particularly for the intellectual types, mindfulness of the body is at first difficult. It is difficult to know what it is all about, what in fact one is supposed to be doing. But once we begin to get the feel of it, it becomes very simple. We forget about it of course, maybe for hours on end, then suddenly the memory returns, and we begin again. 'Happy is he who dwells mindful of the body,' it has been said. Whenever we become tense, nervous, exhausted, if we can remember the 'feel' of mindfulness of the body and re-establish it, the tension and weariness dissolve.

When we find ourselves becoming too relaxed and complacent, then is the time to move on to the second foundation of mindfulness. (Not that the four are to be practised in strictly water-tight compartments, but it is probably wisest to become fairly conversant with one before setting out on the next.) Mindfulness of the feelings requires us to take up a similarly quiet and detached attitude towards our feelings as towards our bodies. By feelings is meant here the emotional reaction that follows any stimulus: pleasure, pain or indifference. We can watch this reaction occurring in response to both physical and mental stimuli. A warm wind blows, the reaction is pleasant; our pride is trampled on, the reaction is painful; we succeed in accomplishing a difficult task, the reaction is pleasant; we get angry about something, the reaction is painful; etc., etc. Again we must be careful not to adopt an objective, mechanistic attitude towards feelings; that would be as erroneous as our old method of clinging passionately to them. What is required is that we watch the arising and the passing away of each feeling—without trying to hold on to it, if it is pleasant, or trying to hurry it away, if it is unpleasant. Gradually we find that our sense of perspective is developing; we no longer identify ourselves with each fleeting feeling or let it carry us away to say or do things that we later regret. It is not at all a question of suppressing any feelings that arise—that would be completely at variance with the practice of mindfulness. But we watch each feeling arise, and, without tampering with it, let it pass away.

Mindfulness of the mind seems to be something of a tautology, yet it is perfectly feasible. In this third foundation of mindfulness we watch the constantly changing quality of the state of mind. Now the mind is joyful, limpid, enthusiastic; now it has become clouded over, sullen, lethargic; now it is sentimental, now reflective, now angry, now compassionate. Always the same advice: watch, do not tamper, allow each state to come and go unimpeded.

The fourth foundation of mindfulness is the most difficult but the most fruitful. Here we relate the object of mindfulness to some aspect of the teaching. For example, if our expectations are suddenly frustrated, instead of noting that there is present an unpleasant feeling or an angry state of mind, we note that there is present suffering (*dukkha*)—the first noble truth. As one mood replaces another, we note *anicca*—impermanence, and so on.

At the end of this book the entire *Satipaṭṭhāna Sutta*, listing in detail the various practices, is given. One more aspect might, however, be mentioned here. The factor of mindfulness is to be developed not only internally but also externally. Mindfulness of the body is to be practised externally as mindfulness of the physical world; again we are not asked to classify or explain, to judge or correct, but only to observe—colour, texture, sound, etc. Mindfulness of feelings and of states of mind can be practised externally by watching their arising and their passing away in other people. And the fourth foundation of mindfulness is potentially present everywhere we look: the sun shifting fitfully through the window, a car passing by in the street, a child eating sweets.

8. *Sammā samādhi*. Right concentration or meditation is the last factor of the path leading to the cessation of suffering. Meditation and its counterpart in daily life—mindfulness (*sati*)—form together the essence of the Buddha's teaching. The third

section of this book will discuss in some detail the various methods and aims of meditation. Here we shall confine ourselves to a few general remarks.

It has been said of the mind that it is like a pool. Too often that pool is agitated and muddy, reflecting nothing but its own turbidity. Buddhist meditation is designed to quieten the mind until it becomes perfectly still. Then the deep recesses of the pool can be seen clearly, and it will reflect a true picture of whatever is presented to it. There are many hindrances in the way of one who seeks to quieten the mind in this way: violent emotions of desire or of hatred, restlessness and discontent, hesitation and doubt, laziness, weariness and sloth. Meditation manuals list the different obstacles that are likely to arise and explain how each one can be dealt with.

Sammā samādhi (right concentration) should not be equated with what the Christian Church calls meditation. Certain elements are, of course, similar, but *sammā samādhi* includes also those states which the Christian would call contemplation rather than meditation. Whether Buddhist *samādhi* goes even beyond contemplation as it is known to the Christian Church—though not, of course, to some of its mystics—or whether it falls short of that goal, is for each one of us to decide, in the light of our own experience.

Part Three
Meditation

IX
Preliminary Instructions for Meditation

In devising a structural pattern for this book, we have departed from the conventional Eastern order of presentation. The teaching of the Buddha has been habitually taught under three headings:

sīla morality
samādhi meditation
paññā wisdom.

In preparing a book designed for the West, we felt it would be more appropriate to outline Buddhist philosophy before discussing its systems of meditation. In a sense this is putting the cart before the horse, the goal before the method. It seemed to us, however, that the Western reader generally likes to have some idea where he is going before learning how to get there. Yet though he may now be intellectually interested in, or even convinced by, the teachings of the Buddha, the reader cannot in fact begin to realize or know the truth of what the Buddha taught until he has experienced it, probably with the help of meditational practices, in his own life.

It has been frequently said that without a teacher one cannot progress far in the practice of meditation. Certain crucial stages—if one is to pass through them satisfactorily—undoubtedly call for either an exceptional degree of self-awareness or an experienced and conscientious teacher. Many self-taught meditators, on reaching one of these crisis periods, abandon the practice altogether, or go off at a tangent and spend the rest of their lives following some fruitless mirage of their own devising. The writers on Christian mysticism have emphasized the need for a spiritual director if the pitfalls and temptations of the contemplative life are to be avoided. So with Buddhist meditation: one is likely to spend a lot of time chasing down blind alleys, one is prey to innumerable temptations —pride, laziness, conceit, self-deception, and so on. Why, then, do we propose to set forth here some of the methods and aims of meditation?

Firstly, although the hazards are inescapable, they are not continuous, and we feel that those who read this book will be in little danger if they try honestly to put the instructions into practice. There is a saying in the East: when the pupil is ready, the teacher will appear. If any readers of this book follow the methods herein outlined until the first crucial stage is reached, a teacher will no doubt appear to help them through it.

Secondly, it is our hope that some will use this book merely as a travel brochure, and will be prompted by it to set out and look for the teacher who will be their guide.

Before discussing the various types of meditation, we propose to list the main preliminary instructions. These apply to all types of meditation and should be carefully considered before any attempt is made to launch out on a specific meditation subject.

1. Choice of a suitable place. This should be quiet, if possible, since—at least in the early stages—noise is likely to be a disturbance. If one's circumstances permit, a special room can be set aside for meditation; in time this room may acquire a certain meditational atmosphere that will enable one more quickly to put aside extraneous thoughts and concentrate on the chosen subject. Certainly it will be found advisable to meditate in the same place whenever possible. Meditation out-of-doors can be a very satisfactory experience and somehow more in harmony with the original teaching.

2. Choice of a suitable time. Unless there is some insurmountable obstruction, the same time each day should be reserved for one's meditation practice. Probably early in the morning or at night would be the most convenient. (Some say that noon is highly propitious, others favour 12 midnight to 3 a.m.!) Regu-

larity is essential. Five minutes every day is of more value than one hour every couple of weeks.

Anyone who has studied a musical instrument will appreciate the validity of these suggestions. If one's meditation practice, like one's piano practice, is done regularly, at the same time every day, the mind begins to prepare for the session beforehand; in this way much less time during the practice session is wasted in 'warming up'.

3. Choice of a suitable posture. Having established a time and a place, we must next choose a suitable sitting posture. It is not necessary to sit in the full lotus posture on a new straw mat, but the position we choose must be comfortable (in time it will be necessary to be able to hold this same posture for an hour or longer). The spine should be straight but not rigid. Hands placed, palms upwards, with the right resting on the left.

These instructions may sound a little weird and magical to the uninitiated. In fact they are based on centuries of experience and observation, and are designed to ensure that the various nerve centres and energy currents of the body are arranged in the most efficient manner.

4. Duration of the practice. Here we come to the most essential factor in the preliminary instructions. A conscious decision should be made as to how long we intend to practise; this may be only five or ten minutes to begin with. It is essential to make this decision and keep to it. The mind will concoct all manner of excuses to tempt us to abandon the project one, two or three minutes before the allocated time is over. These temptations must be firmly resisted. Later we shall find that these temptations to abandon the practice frequently herald a wave of intensified concentration during which the most valuable meditation experiences arise. Unless we form the habit of holding out until the end of the session, we shall never achieve much.

If it is absolutely necessary to stop the practice before the allotted time is up, another conscious decision should be made 'to put down the practice at this time and take it up again later'.

It is imperative that there be no feelings of guilt attendant upon our stopping the practice prematurely, and a deliberate decision to put it aside for a time and then to take it up again will help prevent such feelings from arising.

The length of time devoted to the practice should be gradually but consistently increased until we can 'sit' for an hour. This has been found to be the optimum length for one meditation session.

X
Subjects for Meditation

The first type of meditation which we shall consider is the group of practices designed to correct imbalances in the character.

Buddhist psychology recognizes six dominant character drives, the first three being *akusala* (unskilful or unhealthy) and the second three being *kusala* (skilful or healthy). These drives are usually translated as:

1. Lust — desire for pleasures, past, present and future; greediness, selfishness.

2. Hatred — the tendency to reject, to wish to destroy; hatred can range all the way from sarcasm to brutality.

3. Delusion — the inability to distinguish between that which leads to happiness and that which leads to sorrow; ignorance.

4. Faith — the tendency to trust others, to have confidence in oneself, to seek out that which is wholesome.

5. Wisdom — the tendency to see clearly without cynicism or sentimentality.

6. Discursiveness — versatility of interests; also the ability to handle concepts.

A considerable number of meditation subjects have been found to be useful in weakening the three unhealthy drives and promoting the healthy ones.

Probably the meditation practice most needed in the world at the moment is the meditation on *mettā*. We shall now describe this practice in some detail.

The aim of the meditation on *mettā* is to weaken hatred, replacing it with friendliness and love. Having carried out the preliminary instructions (see Chapter IX), the meditator brings his mind to bear on the subject of friendliness. Although in the beginning it may be found necessary to *think* about friendliness— what it means, why it is desirable, and how it can be put into effect in our lives—the practice itself is not really a matter of conceptual thought. Nor is it a matter of nostalgic, sentimental day-dreaming, Utopia-building. What is required, rather, is that the meditator allows to arise within himself a longing for well-being. As the meditation progresses this longing will become deeper, increasingly mature and realistic.

Mettā has been described as the feeling which a mother has for her child. It is this feeling that the meditator evokes, allowing it to suffuse his whole being until he is surrounded by a sphere of love and benevolence. It is characteristic of the practical approach of Buddhism that the meditation on *mettā* begins with oneself. He is asked to try to begin to love himself. Only when he has succeeded in this, can he begin to love his neighbour, whether enemy or friend, as himself. That this task is an arduous one has been recognized by modern psychology; that it is a fundamental prerequisite for morality, charity and any satisfactory interpersonal relationship is self-evident. Unless we can begin to love ourselves, not blindly and selfishly, but with insight and compassion, we cannot hope to understand, love or help anyone else.

Once the meditator begins to feel that his self-hatred is relaxing, that he is beginning to be concerned about himself and his own well-being, he can embark on the second part of the practice. This consists in spreading the *mettā* outwards from the central point, which is oneself, until it embraces the whole world. Various methods for doing this have been expounded.

(*a*) After suffusing ourselves with loving kindness, we can call to mind our closest friends and relations and try to extend the sphere of our *mettā* to include them. Again it must be stressed that, if the meditation is being correctly practised, there is present neither sentimentality nor possessiveness. A clear sighted, compassionate concern and an earnest desire for the well-being of those we love is what is required. Next, we can extend the sphere of *mettā* to include those whom we hardly know, acquaintances, people we meet in the course of the day. That same concern which we have learned to feel for ourselves and for our closest friends, is now allowed to develop towards those people who 'mean nothing to us'. Finally it is the turn of our enemies— whether they be the latest national bogey-man, the family blacksheep, the income-tax representative, the business rival, or the cock-sure man next door. Here we must be very careful and very honest. We must be careful to avoid mealy-mouthed 'charitable thoughts' that penetrate no further than the surface of our minds; we must be honest in recognizing who our enemies are—or rather who are the people who cause the most hatred to arise within us. It may well be that the multi-murderer featured in the daily newspapers, for whom we think we feel a strong aversion, is in fact less repugnant to us than the woman in the corner store who treats us in a disdainful manner. If the practice of *mettā* is to bear fruit in our lives, everyone for whom we feel aversion—including the lady in the shop at the corner—must be brought within the field of our love and concern.

(*b*) Another method of spreading *mettā* is to radiate it spatially. Having surrounded ourselves with a sphere of loving-kindness, we begin to let this sphere expand until it embraces the whole house where we are sitting. Everyone within the house is included in our longing for happiness and well-being. The practice is further extended to include the street, the city, the country, and ever outward until the entire world is brought within the sphere of *mettā*.

Both these methods are useful. Each has its particular advantages and its particular pitfalls. The teacher-less meditator will have to experiment for himself to see which method is better suited for his own needs, which method is more effective in promoting a deep and lasting cure for his troubled and twisted state of mind. Always one must strive after honesty, not being content with pseudo-feelings and superficial remedies. Always one must be wary if results come too easily or too quickly. Weeding out a habit that has been years in the making will take much time and much effort. If it seems to us that a few hours or a few weeks of practising *mettā* have eradicated a life-long tendency to reject, to abuse and to scorn others, then we had better look a little closer and a little more critically at our new 'friendliness'.

It is not difficult for the Western meditator to realize the need for and the value of the practice of *mettā*. It has somewhat similar counterparts in the formal meditations of the Roman Catholic tradition, and it is easy to fit *mettā* into the context of a Christian way of thinking. Yet it is unlikely that intellectual familiarity with the concept of *mettā*, *caritas* or *agape* will make the task of developing this state of mind any easier. The results, if they are to be lasting, will probably come slowly and falteringly. In spite of the difficulties and frustrations, however, the meditator is not likely to abandon this practice once he has really become attuned to it. 'For in the face of all aridity and disenchantment (love) is as perennial as the grass.'

We do not propose to list and explain here all the many Buddhist meditation subjects designed to correct imbalance in the character. There are a number of meditation manuals which describe in detail these various practices and illustrate the means whereby one can detect the deficiencies and excesses in the character that need remedying.

What we shall do, however, is give a short exposé of four of these character-correcting meditation subjects which are to be practised consecutively. In this case it is not suggested that an hour be spent on each subject! All that is intended is that a short time—perhaps just five minutes for each—be devoted to these four meditation subjects every morning.

If practised in this way, these subjects can be a useful indication of one's state of mind on waking. With experience we can learn to interpret the quality of the various sections of this meditation, and thereby have some foreknowledge of the dominant moods, the weaknesses and strengths that are likely to be in evidence during the day.

1. The first of these meditations is the 'recollection of the triple gem'. This consists in recollecting the Buddha, Dhamma and Sangha (see pp. 25–6). This meditation is one of the more devotional of the Buddhist meditation subjects, although—as we explained earlier—there is no question here of seeking salvation from an outside agency.

The meditator calls to mind the many qualities of the Buddha, frequently using the following formula:

For these reasons is he called Blessed: he is without trace of impurity, he is through his own efforts completely enlightened, he is endowed both with knowledge and with the strength of character to make that knowledge operative, he has passed through the whirlpool of suffering to happiness, he has vision into the various states of existence, more than any other he is able to goad men—providing the will is ready—to continue their search, he is the teacher of men and of those who have gained access to the happier worlds of the devas; for these reasons is he called Buddha, blessed. [1]

In recollecting these attributes of the Buddha, the meditator is not asked merely to sit and worship from afar. If there is value in calling to mind the qualities of another it is so that one may grow in the knowledge of those qualities, gradually incorporating them

[1] A., I, pp. 180, 188, 207, 222; V, pp. 15, 183; D., II, p. 93; M., I, pp. 37, 69, 285, 290, 356, 400, 502; S., II, pp. 69, IV, 304, V, 197, 199, 343, 352 *passim in the Buddhist canon.*

into one's life. The Buddha was no god, nor the son of a god; he was a human being, no different from ourselves; and to those states which he attained we too, by our own efforts, may come.

The meditator next turns to consider the Dhamma which, in this case, means the teaching of the Buddha. He recollects the clarity and consistency of the teaching, remembering the many examples he has encountered in his own life where the teaching has proved accurate and reliable. The teaching is not limited by time, it is of universal validity. It is concerned with the present moment.

The Dhamma guides a man on his way, yet, if that man is wise, he will realize that he must walk the path himself; no one else can follow the Dhamma for him.

Next, the Sangha. The meditator now considers what sort of behaviour is required from a person who is a follower of the Buddha; he considers, too, the various stages of his progress on the path; and finally he reflects on the ways in which he can support those who are trying to put the Buddha's teaching into practice.

This triple meditation is designed to promote *saddhā*—confidence, trust, faith. By reflecting on the Buddha, Dhamma and Sangha, the meditator is strengthened in his faith that there is a goal to be reached, that there is a way to that goal, and that he—like many past, present and future—is capable of following that way and attaining that goal.

2. The second and third sections are perhaps a little more difficult for the Westerner to appreciate: these are the meditations on the body and on death.

The simplest form of the meditation on the body consists in recollecting the skin, flesh and bones of his own body. The meditator begins by focusing his mind on the skin covering the upper lip; then he allows the mind to travel up across the skin of the face, down the back of the head and on to the feet; then up the front of the legs and body to the lower lip. He then switches his mind to consider the flesh under the skin, following the same route. Next he turns his mind to the skeletal structure of the body. The three stages are then repeated in reverse, ending with the skin, i.e.

skin/flesh/bones/bones/flesh/skin.

It must be noted that this meditation does not just require us to visualize the parts of the body, or to intellectualize about them and air our anatomical knowledge; these practices can be resorted to if the attention begins to falter, but they are not the primary function of the meditation exercise. The meditator is rather required to cause his consciousness to arise in the various areas of the body. This may seem a very curious expression to use but the experience which it attempts to describe is simple and straight-forward. Causing one's consciousness to arise in a certain area of the body is somewhat similar to conscious relaxation exercises. In the meditation practice, however, there is no specific intention to relax, nor, of course, to tense up, but only to become more aware.

The speed at which one mentally moves over the body can be varied. When the concentration slackens, it is advisable to increase the speed, as this will stimulate interest and energy. When the mind becomes quieter, and the concentration is sharper, then the speed can be decreased to allow the meditation to become more detailed.

And the purpose of this strange practice? It is said that the main purpose is to subdue sensuality and 'lusting after the flesh'. For this reason, some have maintained that this meditation is not so essential for the Western Buddhist as it is for the 'sensual oriental'! Whether or not the average European or North American is any less 'lustful' than the inhabitants of the Orient, we leave to the reader to decide. Even if the meditator pleads not guilty to the charge of sensuality, he can still profit from the practice of the meditation on the body. For this meditation will help to stimulate our analytical faculty, and—more important—will contribute to the gradual weakening of possessive tendencies.

3. The third meditation is the recollection of death. The meditator is to consider the inevitability and unpredictability of death. He can reflect on the length of his present life: maybe he has forty years to live before death comes; maybe twenty or ten; maybe only one year of life remains, or a month; maybe this day will be the last day, or this hour; maybe there is just time for one in-breath and one out-breath before death comes. The meditator can consider that the time and the place of his death are still unknown to him; perhaps death will come in summer, or in the spring, in autumn or in winter; maybe at night or at noon, in the evening or with the rising of the sun; maybe he will die at home or in the street, on the sea or in a forest, in his own country or abroad. It is not known whether he will die while he is lying down or whether he will be struck dead as he is standing or walking. The cause of death is not yet known: will it be a disease or a stray bullet, accidental poisoning or old age, a nuclear explosion or a broken heart?

The Buddhist meditation on death is not at all a morbid thing. Its purpose is to stimulate energy and a sense of urgency. It is designed also to weaken the tendency to possessiveness and craving. And finally it imparts a certain balance to life. As far as possible in the modern world death has been covered up; the dead body is whisked away, washed and perfumed, and clothed in fresh garments, before anyone can see it; coffins are luxurious, cemeteries are gardens of rest. It is not etiquette to mention death or decay. We are all expected to live as though death, which is the one inescapable certainty, did not exist. This self-deception and artificiality contrasts violently with the simple sanity of the Middle Ages, when a skull was set in the centre of the feast table, or of Roman times, when, as the victorious general was led in triumph through the streets of Rome, a man at his side whispered constantly to him 'Remember you are only mortal'.

By practising the recollection on death, we can restore some balance to our lives. Without becoming paranoid or hypochondriacs, we can begin to live with the ever-present awareness of

Plates

1. The Buddha: Daibutsu, Nara, Japan

2. The Buddha—from Sarnath, India

3. *Above: Mahābodhi* Vihāra,
'*Bodhi*' tree and *Vajrāsana*,
Buddagaya, India, *right:*
Mūlagandhakuti Vihāra,
Sarnah, India

4. *Left:* The Buddha—from Mathura, India, *right:* The Buddha at Galvihāra, Polonnaruva, Ceylon

5. *Right:* Samādhipratimā of the Buddha
—from Anuradhapura, Ceylon,
below: The Buddha—from Toluvila,
Ceylon

Right: The Buddha—from Vehera-gala, Ceylon, *below:* The Buddha—from Lopburi, Thailand

7. *Left:* Buddha head—from Japan, *right:* The Buddha—from Japan

death. Far from undermining our happiness or our vitality, this awareness will give a hitherto unrealized depth and value to life itself.

4. The last of these meditations is *mettā*. This practice has already been described at the beginning of the chapter. Here we shall only consider its rôle in the context of these four meditations.

The first meditation—on the Buddha, Dhamma and Sangha—stimulates faith, joy, self-confidence. Lest this joy and confidence be turned to unprofitable (*akusala*) ends, the second meditation—on the parts of the body—encourages us to analyse that which we usually hold so precious. The third meditation—on death—is designed to promote energy and the will to get on with the job in hand. This in turn is tempered by the fourth meditation, which teaches us not to separate ourselves from the rest of humanity when we embark on our task of self-liberation.

XI
Samatha Meditation

Buddhist meditation is divided into two categories:

samatha the development of calm and concentration; and
vipassanā the development of insight.

Samatha meditation encompasses all that which in the Christian Church goes under the heading of miracles and visions, its subjects being *fixed* objects, either internal or external. At the beginning, especially if one is working without a teacher, external subjects are perhaps more suitable.

Possibly the best-known and most frequently practised of the external *samatha* meditation subjects are the four colour *kasiṇas*. The practice of *kasiṇa* meditation requires us first to construct a *kasiṇa*, or disc, of the chosen colour—red, white, yellow or blue. The ancient meditation manuals explain the exact quality and tone of the stipulated colours; they explain too how the would-be meditator should fashion his *kasiṇa*: as with the much later development of Zen flower arrangements and tea ceremonies, the preparation of the *kasiṇa* should be an integral part of the meditation; every action should be carried out with quiet awareness and relaxed precision. The size of the disc may vary; some say the diameter should measure the same as the hand span of the meditator plus the width of our fingers; others say that the size of the *kasiṇa* should be modified according to the degree of concentration present in the meditator: those of dull concentration using larger discs, and those of sharp concentration smaller ones.

The disc should be set up at a reasonable distance from the meditator. Here again the sources differ in the distances they recommend. Probably about ten to fifteen feet will be found to be satisfactory. The centre of the disc should be slightly lower than the horizontal eye level of the meditator when he is seated in front of the *kasiṇa*.

Having constructed the *kasiṇa*, placed it in a suitable spot and seated himself before it, the meditator can begin the practice proper. The gaze should be allowed to focus on the disc, without staring or in any way straining the vision. After a few seconds, the eyes are closed but the concentration remains focused on the memory of the disc. If a disc appears while the eyes are closed— as, for example, when we look for a second at the moon and then close our eyes—the meditator should concentrate on that until it fades. The process is then repeated until the allotted time for the meditation session is over. The meditator will probably find that sometimes he is able to hold the image of the disc much longer than at other times. All these things should be noted; with ex- perience it will become possible to relate the various states and sequences of one's meditation session to one's habits and character traits.

A more elaborate form of *kasiṇa* meditation is the *maṇḍala*. A *maṇḍala* consists of a symmetrical pattern which is used as an aid to concentration in much the same way as the *kasiṇa*. *Maṇḍalas* are usually many-coloured, and frequently depict symbolic or mythological figures arranged in an intricate and stylized pattern. Many of the Indian and Tibetan works of art now seen on display in the West were originally fashioned as *maṇḍalas*, and used by monks in their meditation practices.

The meditation practice most respected by Buddhists—it was the practice used by the Buddha on the night of his enlightenment —is that of *ānāpānasati*. *Ānāpānasati*—the recollection of in- breathing and out-breathing—is, as it were, a universal medita- tion subject. It is recommended as a character-correcting practice; it is one of the foremost *samatha* (calming) subjects and it is per- haps the most natural—if not the most spectacular—of *vipassanā* (insight) meditation subjects.

We shall here consider the use of *ānāpānasati* as a *samatha* subject. The meditator is asked to focus his attention at the tip of the nostrils. A word of warning may be given: it is not necessary to squint (mentally) and focus the closed eyes on the nostrils; the gaze of the closed eyes can be directed in a relaxed manner straight ahead; it is the mind or consciousness which is 'focused' on the tip of the nostrils. Then, we quietly watch the breath flowing in and out past the tip of the nostrils. It is sometimes found useful to count the breaths, as this may help to anchor the concentration. Various methods of counting may be employed. Usually it is not recommended to count beyond ten, and if the concentration is broken, the meditator should begin again at one. It is essential to remember that it is not the counting that matters, but the continuity of the concentration on the breath.

As with the *kasiṇa* practice, the meditator practising *anāpānasati* should carefully observe everything that happens during the meditation session: whether the in-breath or the out-breath is clearer; whether this remains constant throughout the session, or whether there is a change in the pattern; whether the concentration is keener at the beginning or at the end of the practice; and so on.

Finally, in this brief survey of *samatha* meditation subjects, we should mention the practice of repeating a word or sequence of words. This type of practice will be familiar to those who have some knowledge of the meditation systems of the Greek Orthodox Church. The 'Jesus prayer' or the 'prayer of the heart', is much used by monks of the Greek Orthodox faith.

With all forms of *samatha* meditation, the chosen subject, whether it be the breathing, a coloured disc, or the repetition of a special phrase, is only a stepping stone, or an aid to concentration. The meditator focuses his attention on the chosen subject until the mind becomes quiet and one-pointed. At this stage a conceptual image (*nimitta*) will arise. Buddhist literature abounds in description of various types of *nimitta*: essentially it is a 'sign' that appears in front of the closed eyes. If the meditator was using a *kasina* subject, then the *nimitta* that eventually arises will probably take the form of a disc. If the *ānāpānasati* practice was used, then the *nimitta* may take the form of a wisp of smoke or a flurry of clouds. If the 'formulated utterance' practice—*araham sammāsambuddho* (free from all impurity, by his own efforts completely enlightened)—was being repeated, then the resultant *nimitta* may be a vision of a Buddha statue or painting. Or—to apply Buddhist terminology to the practices of the Christian contemplatives—if a *mandala* consisting of an image of Christ is used as a *samatha* meditation subject, then the *nimitta* that will arise may well be a 'vision' of that same Christ. Buddhism, however, recognizes no divine intervention in the case of such visions. A *nimitta* arises in the mind when a certain degree of concentration has been reached. The *nimitta*—however holy or awe-inspiring its appearance—is a perfectly natural occurrence, the *vipāka*, as it were, of a certain *kammic* development. Anyone, providing he carry out the necessary preparatory work, can 'see visions' and 'dream dreams' without supernatural assistance.

Once the *nimitta* has arisen before the closed eyes of the meditator—and it may take months or years of conscientious practice before this moment comes!—he abandons the previous subject of his *samatha* practice, and focuses the mind on the *nimitta*. Care must be taken at this point not to chase *nimittas*! If it seems to be floating up out of sight, remain calm and quiet, and keep the attention focused in the central point where the *nimitta* first arose. If this is done, it will soon 'float' back into place. (If, on the contrary, like Alice one allows the mind to go chasing up after the *nimitta*, it will disappear out of the roof—like the articles in the shop owned by the sheep.)

While concentrating on the *nimitta* one must be careful to keep the attention taut—neither too slack nor too tense. If the attention seems to be getting too slack, we can begin to observe the *nimitta* more precisely: its exact colour, texture, shape; whether it is increasing or decreasing in size, etc. If the attention becomes too tense, on the other hand, we should refrain from much 'observation' and merely let the mind rest in the centre of the *nimitta*.

There are three main benefits to be derived from *samatha* meditation.

Firstly, the meditator will find that something of the calm and concentration attained during his daily meditation session will carry over into the rest of the day. The problems of life will not, of course, have been solved but he will begin to feel more capable of dealing with them. As a central point of tranquillity becomes established in him, he will find that he is endowed with a new sense of proportion and perspective. Fears, disappointments, irritations, hopes, surprises and shocks will not cease to affect him, but their impact will be cushioned by his inner calm and he will be less likely to be goaded by them into untimely speech or action. If the meditator notices that his meditation sessions are improving dramatically—he is attaining trance-like states of concentration—and yet there is no change in his daily life itself, he should be very wary and examine carefully the content and quality of his meditation sessions. It may well be that what he has been calling tranquillity and concentration is, in fact, a state of self-induced hypnotism. The latter, though interesting as a mental phenomenon, has no place in the context of Buddhist meditation, nor is it of any value to those seeking an answer to the problems of human malaise.

The other two benefits of *samatha* meditation are much more difficult to attain. In Christian terminology we might call them (1) ecstatic trances and (2) miracles.

An ecstatic trance, or *jhāna*, has been analysed and systematized by Buddhist scholars. The various stages of *jhāna* have been recognized and named, and the line between the visionary and mystic experiences demarcated. We shall outline here the sequence of events that precedes the attainment of the first *jhāna* (the most elementary ecstatic trance); this same sequence is then repeated on a higher plane of consciousness as the various stages of *jhāna* are traversed.

Firstly, the thought processes are regulated until they revolve around a single theme. The revolutions are narrowed down until the thought remains focused on the central point. From this stage onward there is a dropping of conceptual thought in favour of pure awareness—experience rather than verbalization. There is an acute sense of pleasurable interest that is gradually refined. Joy arises and quiet happiness. The mind becomes completely one-pointed, free from all division, conflict and confusion. Finally there is a breakthrough to another sphere of consciousness, known to Buddhists as the first *jhāna* and to Christians as an ecstatic trance. The attainment of *jhāna* brings a state of unparalleled bliss, the effects of which can be felt in life for some time afterwards.

We shall consider now the Buddhist attitude towards those actions which the Christian would call miracles: walking on water, levitation and the like. Experience has shown that these feats are not brought about through divine intervention into affairs but are the natural outcome of a certain type of human development. Buddhist meditation manuals list the various phychic powers (*iddhis*) towards which the *samatha* meditator can, if he wish, work. Specific subjects are recommended for developing specific 'miraculous' powers. As a prerequisite the meditator has to become thoroughly proficient in the various *jhānas*, be able to enter them at will and in whatever order he chooses.

Although the continued and conscientious practice of *samatha* meditation can lead to the development of miraculous powers, the meditator is warned of the dangers attendant on such attainments. If his spiritual growth is not to be adversely affected he must take care never to boast of his achievements or display them to others (unless within the community of monks). It is in harmony with this attitude that Christ rejected the devil's second temptation. That Christ had the power, developed by some form of meditational practice, to fling himself unharmed from the pinnacle of the temple is beyond doubt. That he refused to do so proves the soundness of his spiritual training. By performing this 'miracle' Christ could have saved himself much trouble and convinced the people of his 'divinity'. He knew, however, that faith induced by miracles is not true faith and that his followers must come to him by the slow way of their own experience.

Similarly it is in accord with the warning expressed in meditation manuals—not to use psychic power for one's personal satisfaction or gratification—that Christ rejected the temptation to turn stone into bread.

The results, both spectacular and intimate, of *samatha* meditation raise many questions and doubts in the mind of the meditator. How long can a man dare to live in the blissful *jhāna* world, when the basic problem of human suffering has not been solved? How deeply can one delve into the wonders of psychic power without falling captive to its dangers? The temptation to use meditation experiences for personal, political or 'religious' ends—rather than just observing them as indications that one has attained a high degree of concentration—this temptation is difficult to resist. The third temptation of Christ was the temptation of political power; the annals of the Churches record many examples of Christian zealots who were less wary than their founder.

For the true follower of the Buddha, the ability to perform miracles and see visions is but a side product of meditation; it may be gratifying and ecstatically pleasurable but it does not bring one any nearer to the goal—which is the release from the cause of suffering. The branch of Buddhist meditation which deals exclusively with this problem—with the development of insight and thence of freedom—is called *vipassanā*. It is *vipassanā* meditation that we shall consider in the final chapter of this book.

XII
Vipassanā Meditation

Vipassanā meditation is based on the principles of *sati*, or mindfulness (see pp. 54–56), and in order to bear full fruit must be practised in conjunction with right mindfulness, the seventh factor of the path. The subjects of *vipassanā* meditation are all moving objects, internal or external. In discussing the development of *sati* we listed several of these objects, any of which can be used for the practice of *vipassanā* meditation. Here again the simplest and possibly most effective subject is *ānāpānasati*, the recollection of in-breathing and out-breathing.

The practice is begun in the same way as for *samatha* meditation. The attention is focused on the tip of the nostrils and the meditator observes the passage of the breath in and out. Here, however, the emphasis is slightly different. Whereas in *samatha* meditation the attention is centred on a point at the tip of the nostrils past which the breath flows, in *vipassanā* meditation the subject is the moving breath. In the early stages of the practice of *ānāpānasati* no clear distinction can be made between the two forms; or, to speak more accurately, in the early stages of meditation, when the mind is still uncontrolled and restless, the only course open to the meditator will be to practise *samatha*. Later, when concentration and calm have been developed, he will be in a position to choose whether he wishes to continue on to the higher stages of *samatha* meditation or set out on the way of *vipassanā*.

Vipassanā meditation demands a much more analytical and probing approach. Here, the mind is not encouraged to bathe in the bliss of quiet concentration on a (seemingly) stable object but is driven to question more deeply and observe more closely. Which is the clearest, the beginning, middle or end of the in-breath? And of the out-breath? What happens during the pause? Is there a pause? Similar questions are asked at first in the *samatha* practice but there the purpose is only to help anchor the restless thoughts; once the mind is fairly quiet, questioning is abandoned in favour of calm contemplation. In the practice of *vipassanā*, however, the mind is not allowed to rest but is constantly questioned and goaded to look more carefully into the appearance of things.

If during the practice of *vipassanā* meditation, a *nimitta* arises, it is not a sign for rejoicing—as in *samatha* meditation; here it is merely watched and allowed to fade. Indeed, whatever ecstatic or terrifying visions arise, they are cause neither for joy nor for fear. They should not be clung to, nor rejected. Just watch them appear, live for a certain time, and then pass away.

The same is true for any disturbances to the meditation, whether these disturbances are external (noises or smells, etc.) or internal (pains, itching, stray thoughts, etc.). In *samatha* meditation, disturbances are avoided as far as possible and ignored if they arise. In *vipassanā* meditation 'disturbances' are in fact impossible, since whatever is the present object of consciousness —whether it be the barking of a dog, the painful feeling in the foot, or the movement of the breath—automatically becomes the meditation subject. A sound impinges on the ear, the meditator merely notes 'hearing' and the sensation passes; he notes the arising and passing away of any emotional or intellectual responses occasioned by the 'hearing', and then immediately switches back to the original subject, *ānāpānasati*. The thought of food arises, he notes merely 'thinking' or 'wanting' and watches the thought or the desire gradually fade.

The practice of *vipassanā* meditation is rigorous and exhausting. Without a competent teacher it is difficult, since the mind prefers the quiet patterns of *samatha* practice. *Vipassanā* demands a ruthless honesty and a deep-rooted conviction that this is the way. Without this honesty the mind will avoid the real, existential questions and will wander off into by-ways of intellectual speculation. Without conviction (*saddhā*) the meditator will be unable to maintain throughout the day that minimum degree of mindfulness necessary if the *vipassanā* practice is to come to fulfilment. The result of *vipassanā* mediation is insight, various stages and degrees of insight; and from insight is born freedom.

The various truths or insights that arise during the practice of *vipassanā* are not 'known' by the rational, intellectual mind but by experience. One does not think about *anicca*, work it out, and decide that it must be true; this intellectual activity is stimulating and necessary, but it is not *vipassanā* meditation. Instead, one watches the arising and passing away of the meditation subject until suddenly there is *anicca*—and there is no 'me' separate from it.

According to Theravāda Buddhism (the Southern school of Ceylon, Thailand, Burma, etc.), it is the practice of *vipassanā* that leads to the attainment of the Path—or, as the Zen masters would call it, *Satori*. Almost from the first hours of his practice of *vipassanā* the meditator will find that 'insights' arise; he will begin to see himself and the world in a new light; he will recognize relationships and sequences, where previously there was only a disjointed jumble of impressions; his awareness of detail will become more acute and his appreciation of structure more subtle. And as each new insight arises, a further stage of freedom will be realized. The meditator will find the bonds of self centred ignorance gradually loosening. After a certain time, which may be hours or life-times, these insights build up to a climax. The experience of Path-consciousness that results is in some respects similar to the experience of a deep state of meditation (*jhāna*). In both cases there is a break through to another plane of consciousness but there the similarity ends. Whereas *jhāna* is a temporary escape from the sorrow and unsatisfactoriness of human existence, the path-moment is a permanent release.

Theravāda Buddhism maintains that the experience of the

Path must occur four times before total liberation is attained. At each of the four stages certain specific fetters—that bind men to the wheel of rebirth—are weakened or destroyed. With the final, fourth stage of the Path, the last remnants of ignorance are uprooted and a state of complete enlightenment ensues.

The practice of *vipassanā* meditation and the development of *sati* are, according to the teaching of the Southern school, the surest and most direct way to the enlightenment experience. As such they may well be called the heart of Buddhist meditation, indeed the heart of the entire teaching.

Conclusion

Buddhism has come to the West in various guises. From the scientific Buddhism of the late nineteenth century to the Beat Zen of the mid-twentieth century, there have been as many different presentations of the teaching as there have been 'gurus' presenting it. Freud said of religion that it is a collective neurosis; a few years ago in England, Buddhism was tending to become a collective psychosis, a socially acceptable schizophrenia. It might be of value here to study briefly this strange phenomenon, for if we are to be successful in our search for a vital interpretation of Buddhism, it is as well for us to know some of the peculiarly Western pitfalls into which we may be drawn.

In the tense, nerve-racking climate of European or North American civilization, it is easy for the 'way' to become a systematic, unrelieved, clinical observation of the body and the mind as intricate mechanisms devoid of 'soul'. With diabolical persistence, the devotee can shatter his own beingness into a myriad objective 'its'—impersonal functions and complex patterns of behaviour. Eagerly he will submit himself to long periods of rigorous discipline, maintaining a minimum of twenty hours meditation a day for weeks or even months. While engaged on this practice, once the initial wrench with the world has been made, one is cool and clear, one is omnipotent and impregnable; one lives and moves and has one's being in the isolated safety of the ascetic's padded cell. This isolation and schizoid depersonalization contrasts violently with the warmth and humanity that pervades much of the scriptures. The early monks were exhorted to strive earnestly, to meditate ceaselessly, to work out their own salvation with diligence; but their life was not one of an isolated robot in an ivory tower; they trudged through mud and filth begging their food from door to door; they came together to talk and argue with each other—and with monks of different faiths; they are portrayed as individual beings with individual virtues and vices, talents and foibles; they laughed and cried; they squabbled and schemed; and when the day of enlightenment dawned they emerged from the experience not with awful solemnity but with whoops of joy and warmhearted gratitude.

At the other extreme from the over-earnest striver is the drug-happy hippie. Revolted by the hypocrisy and bureaucracy of a society 'they never made', thousands of young people are rejecting any kind of conformity or discipline and throwing themselves into the arms of the nearest 'Zen master'. Instead of the rigours of Zen they find there the solace and the exuberant 'reality' of the psychedelic world. That youth is appalled at the prospect of being swamped by a technocratic society is not in itself an unhealthy sign, but to escape therefrom into the realms of drug-induced visions is neither healthy nor Buddhist—Zen or otherwise.

The Buddha spoke frequently of the various states of existence —the world of spirits, blissful or tormented, the world of unhappy ghosts, the world of animals, the world of men. The Buddha himself is often referred to as one who has vision into the various worlds of existence. Yet repeatedly he taught that it is on the human plane that the long path to liberation is to be undertaken. Other planes may be more blissful, they may indeed be a temporary 'heavenly reward' for meritorious behaviour, but they do not afford the right soil in which the seeds of enlightenment can grow. The conflicts and confusion, the constant, never-satisfied striving for peace and security, the existential anguish that characterize human life are the very stuff of which liberation is made. To escape from this conflict into the LSD experience is but a temporary suspension of our human status. When the trip is over—whether it was to the *deva* (celestial) world of unsurpassed joy or to the drear wastes of the *preta* ('shadow') realm, whether it was a fleeting visit or a lifelong habit—when the trip is over, back we must come to the human world to work out our salvation in the midst of the nuclear arms race and surrounded by our bingo-crazy relations.

The Buddha said: 'I teach but two things—suffering and the release from suffering.'[1] For the child, to be hungry is suffering, to be fed is the release. For the saint, all compounded things are suffering, the uncompounded alone is free from suffering. The Buddhist way of life consists in the gradual maturing and refining of our experience and knowledge of what pleasure and pain, happiness and distress, security and insecurity are.

Buddhism is a gradual path of maturity, leading away from the infantile dependence on the Father to adult integration and interdependence. The emphasis is on the process of adolescence, on the gradual passing through each stage on the way to adulthood. It is with these intermediary stages that we are concerned in our practice of the path, and great care must be taken not to imagine that we are further ahead than we really are.

A German monk once remarked: 'One must strengthen the ego before one can get rid of it'. Too often we are tempted to adopt the theories and ideals of Buddhism, or of any religion, as a defence against the slow, painful process of adolescence. Christ has said that unless one becomes as a little child one cannot enter the kingdom of heaven. But this rebirth as a child comes out of the maturity of adulthood and not out of a failure to attain that maturity. So, too, with the fundamental Buddhist virtue of non-attachment. If we begin with a state of hatred, rejection and despair, we cannot pass immediately from this extreme and begin to cultivate the highest virtue of non-attachment. We should merely pass from an active neurotic state to an equally neurotic passive state. There is a necessary intermediary stage where love replaces hatred, acceptance replaces rejection, and faith replaces fear.

[1] M., I, p. 140.

Appendices

The Foundation of Mindfulness

Thus I have heard:

Once the Buddha was living among the people called Kuru at their market town, Kammāssadamma. There he addressed the monks as follows:

Monks, this is the only way for the purification of beings, for the overcoming of sorrow and lamentation, for the destruction of suffering and grief for reaching the right path, for the attainment of Nibbāna, that is to say the Foundation of Mindfulness.

Monks, here a monk (1) practising contemplation on the body, (2) on feelings, (3) on mind and (4) on phenomena dwells ardent, fully aware and mindful, having got rid of covetousness and grief concerning the world.

(1) How, monks, does a monk dwell practising contemplation on the body?

Monks, here a monk who has betaken himself to a forest, to the foot of a tree or to an empty place, sits down cross-legged, keeps the body erect, establishes mindfulness before him and breathes in and out mindfully.

Breathing in a long breath, he knows, I am breathing in a long breath; or breathing out a long breath, he knows, I am breathing out a long breath; or breathing in a short breath, he knows, I am breathing in a short breath; or breathing out a short breath, he knows, I am breathing out a short breath.

'Conscious of the whole (breath) body, I will breath in', thus, he trains himself. 'Conscious of the whole (breath) body, I will breath out', thus, he trains himself. 'Calming the bodily formation, I will breath in', thus, he trains himself. And 'Calming the bodily formation, I will breath out', thus, he trains himself.

Monks, again, a monk, when walking, knows, I am walking, or standing, knows I am standing, or when sitting, knows, I am sitting, or when lying down, knows, I am lying down, or he knows every position in which he places the body.

Monks, again, in walking to and fro, a monk practises full awareness; in looking ahead, and in looking elsewhere, he practises full awareness; in bending and in stretching, he practises full awareness; in using the outer and other robes, and bowl, he practises full awareness; in eating, drinking, chewing, and tasting, he practises full awareness; in evacuating and in making water, he practises full awareness; and in walking, standing, sitting, sleeping, waking, speaking, and being silent, he practises full awareness.

Monks, again, a monk takes stock of this very body—from the sole of the foot up and from the scalp down, bounded by skin, and full of foul things such as head-hair, body-hair, nails, teeth, skin, sinews, bones, etc.

Monks, again, a monk takes stock, by way of the elements, of this very body according as it is found or placed, thus, in this body there are the elements of earth, water, fire and air.

Monks, again, just as if a monk were seeing a body one day dead, or two days dead, or three days dead, swollen up, blue, and festering, abandoned in a charnel-ground, just so he thinks of his own body: Truly, this body too is of such a nature; such will it become, and it has not escaped that state.

Monks, again, just as if a monk were seeing crows, kites, vultures, dogs, jackals, or various kinds of worms devouring a body abandoned in a charnel-ground, just so he thinks of his own body: Truly, this body too is of such a nature; such it will become; and it has not escaped that state.

Monks, again, just as if a monk were seeing a body abandoned in a charnel-ground, a skeleton held together by sinews with some flesh and blood adhering to it, a fleshless skeleton held together by sinews, a skeleton without flesh and blood but held together by sinews, loose bones scattered in every direction, hand-bones, foot-bones, thigh-bones, pelvis, spine, and skull, here and there, shell-white bones, bones heaped together for more than a year, rotted and crumbling bones, just so he thinks of his own body: Truly this body too is of such nature; such it will become; and it has not escaped that state.

Thus he dwells practising contemplation on the body internally or externally, or both internally and externally.

He dwells practising contemplation of origination or dissolution or both origination and dissolution on the body. Or indeed, the mindfulness that 'there is a body' is established in him for growth in knowledge and mindfulness, and he dwells independent, clinging to nothing in the world.

Thus indeed, monks, a monk dwells practising contemplation on the body.

(2) How, monks, does a monk dwell practising feeling-contemplation on feelings?

Here monks, a monk feeling a pleasant feeling, knows, I feel a pleasant feeling; or feeling a painful feeling, knows, I feel a painful feeling; or feeling a neutral feeling, knows, I feel a neutral feeling; or feeling a pleasant worldly feeling, knows. I feel a pleasant worldly feeling; or feeling a pleasant unworldly feeling, knows, I feel a pleasant unworldly feeling; or feeling a painful worldly feeling knows, I feel a painful worldly feeling; or feeling a painful unworldly feeling, knows, I feel a painful unworldly feeling; or feeling a neutral worldly feeling, knows, I feel a neutral worldly feeling; or feeling a neutral unworldly feeling, knows, I feel a neutral unworldly feeling.

Thus he dwells practising contemplation of origination on feelings internally, or externally, or both internally and externally.

He dwells practising contemplation of origination or dissolution, or both origination and dissolution on feelings. Or indeed, the mindfulness that 'feeling exists' is established in him for growth in knowledge and mindfulness, and he dwells independent clinging to nothing in the world.

Monks, thus indeed a monk dwells practising contemplation on feelings.

(3) And how monks, does a monk dwell practising mind-contemplation on the mind?

Here monks, a monk knows the mind with lust as with lust, or knows the mind without lust as without lust, or knows the mind with hate as with hate, or knows the mind without hate as without hate, or knows the mind with delusion as with delusion or knows the mind without delusion as without delusion, or knows the indolent mind as indolent, or knows the distracted mind as distracted, or knows the mind grown great as grown great, or knows the mind not grown great as not grown great, or knows the surpassable mind as surpassable, or knows the unsurpassable mind as unsurpassable, or knows the concentrated mind as concentrated, or knows the mind not concentrated as not concentrated, or knows the freed mind as freed, or knows the mind not freed as not freed.

Thus he dwells practising mind-contemplation on the mind internally, or externally, or both internally and externally.

He dwells practising origination-contemplation on the mind, or dissolution-contemplation on the mind, or both origination and dissolution-contemplation on the mind. Or indeed, the mindfulness that 'there is the mind' is established in him for growth in knowledge and mindfulness, and he dwells independent clinging to nothing in the world.

Monks, thus indeed, a monk dwells practising mind contemplation on the mind.

(4) And how monks, does a monk dwell practising contemplation on phenomena?

Here monks, a monk dwells practising contemplation on phenomena of the five hindrances.

How monks, does a monk dwell practising contemplation on phenomena of the five hindrances?

Here monks, a monk knows the presence of sensuality within, thus: There is sensuality in me, or he knows the absence of sensuality within, thus, There is no sensuality in me. And how the arising of unarisen sensuality comes to be—that he knows; how the rejection of arisen sensuality comes to be—that he knows and how the absence of future arising of rejected sensuality comes to be—that he knows.

He knows the presence of ill-will within, thus, There is ill-will in me, or he knows the absence of ill will within, thus, There is no ill will in me. And how the arising of unarisen ill-will comes to be—that he knows; and how the absence of future arising of rejected ill-will comes to be—that he knows.

He knows the presence of rigidity and torpor within, thus, There is rigidity and torpor in me, or he knows the absence of rigidity and torpor within, thus, There is no rigidity and torpor in me. And how the arising of unarisen rigidity and torpor comes to be—that he knows; how the rejection of arisen rigidity and torpor comes to be—that he knows; and how the absence of future arising of rejected rigidity and torpor comes to be—that he knows.

He knows the presence of agitation and anxiety within, thus, There is agitation and anxiety in me, or he knows the absence of agitation and anxiety within, thus, There is no agitation and anxiety in me. And how the arising of unarisen agitation and anxiety comes to be—that he knows; how the rejection of arisen agitation and anxiety comes to be—that he knows; and how the absence of future arising of rejected agitation and anxiety comes to be—that he knows.

He knows the presence of uncertainty within, thus, There is uncertainty in me, or he knows the absence of uncertainty within thus, There is no uncertainty in me. And how the arising of unarisen uncertainty comes to be—that he knows; how the rejection of arisen uncertainty comes to be—that he knows; and how the absence of future arising of rejected uncertainty comes to be—that he knows.

Monks, thus indeed, a monk dwells practising contemplation on phenomena of the five hindrances.

Monks, again, a monks dwells practising contemplation on phenomena of the five aggregates of clinging.

How monks, does a monk dwell practising contemplation on phenomena of the five aggregates of clinging?

Here monks, a monk thinks, Thus is matter, thus is the arising of matter, and thus is the passing away of matter; thus is feeling, thus is the arising of feeling, and thus is the passing away of feeling; thus is perception, thus is the arising of perception, and thus is the passing away of perception; thus are formations, thus is the arising of formations, and thus is the passing away of formations; thus is consciousness, thus is the arising of consciousness, and thus is the passing away of consciousness.

Monks, thus indeed, a monk dwells practising contemplation on phenomena of the five aggregates of clinging.

Monks, again, a monk dwells practising contemplation on phenomena of the six internal and external sense-bases.

How monks, does a monk dwell practising contemplation on phenomena of the six internal and external sense-bases?

Here monks, a monk knows the eye, knows visible forms, and knows the fetter that arises depending on both. And how the arising of the unarisen fetter comes to be—that he knows; how the rejection of the arisen fetter comes to be that he knows, and how the absence of future arising of the rejected fetter comes to be—that he knows.

He knows the ear, knows sounds, and knows the fetter that arises depending on both. And how the arising of the unarisen fetter comes to be—that he knows; how the rejection of the arisen fetter comes to be—that he knows; and how the absence of future arising of the rejected fetter comes to be—that he knows.

He knows the nose, knows smells, and knows the fetter that arises depending on both. And how the arising of the unarisen fetter comes to be—that he knows; how the rejection of the arisen fetter comes to be—that he knows; and how the absence of future arising of the rejected fetter comes to be—that he knows.

He knows the tongue; knows tastes, and knows the fetter that arises depending on both. And how the arising of the unarisen fetter comes to be—that he knows; how the rejection of the arisen fetter comes to be—that he knows; and how the absence of future arising of the rejected fetter comes to—that he knows.

He knows the body, knows tactual objects and knows the fetter that arises depending on both. And how the arising of the unarisen fetter comes to be—that he knows; how the rejection of the arisen fetter comes to be that he knows; and how the absence of future arising of the rejected fetter comes to be—that he knows.

He knows the mind, knows phenomena, and knows the fetter that arises depending on both. And how the arising of the unarisen fetter comes to be—that he knows; how the rejection of the arisen fetter comes to be—that he knows; and how the absence of future arising of the rejected fetter comes to be—that he knows.

Monks, thus indeed, a monk dwells practising phenomenon–contemplation on phenomena of the six internal and external sense-bases.

Monks, again a monk dwells practising phenomenon-contemplation on phenomena of the seven factors of enlightenment.

How monks, does a monk dwell practising phenomenon-contemplation on phenomena of the seven factors of enlightenment?

Here monks, a monk knows the presence of the enlightenment-factors of mindfulness, investigation of phenomena, energy, rapture, calm, concentration, and equanimity, within, thus, The enlightenment-factors are in me, or he knows the absence of the enlightenment-factors within, thus, The enlightenment-factors are not in me. And how the arising of the unarisen enlightenment-factors come to be—that he knows; and how the perfecting through development of the arisen enlightenment-factors come to be—that he knows.

Thus he dwells practising phenomenon-contemplation on phenomena internally, or externally, or both internally and externally.

He dwells practising origination-contemplation on phenomena, or dissolution-contemplation on phenomena, or both origination- and dissolution-contemplation on phenomena. Or indeed, the mindfulness that 'there are phenomena' is established in him for growth in knowledge and mindfulness, and he dwells independent, clinging to nothing in the world.

Monks, thus indeed, a monk dwells practising phenomenon-contemplation on phenomena of the seven factors of enlightenment.

Monks, again, a monk dwells practising phenomenon-contemplation on phenomena of the four noble truths.

How monks, does a monk dwell practising phenomenon-contemplation on phenomena of the four noble truths?

Here monks, a monk knows according to fact. This is ill. He knows according to fact, This is the origin of ill. He knows according to fact, This is the cessation of ill. And he knows according to fact, This is the way leading to the cessation of ill.

Thus he dwells practising phenomenon-contemplation on phenomena internally, or externally, or both internally and externally.

He dwells practising origination-contemplation on phenomena, or dissolution-contemplation on phenomena, or both origination- and dissolution-contemplation on phenomena. Or indeed, the mindfulness that 'there are phenomena' is established in him for growth in knowledge and mindfulness, and he dwells independent, clinging to nothing in the world.

Monks, thus indeed, a monk dwells practising phenomenon-contemplation on phenomena of the four noble truths.

Monks, were a monk to develop these four foundations of mindfulness in this manner for seven years, one of two results may be expected in him; knowledge here and now, or, if there be yet an element of clinging, non-return.

Let alone seven years, monks, were a monk to develop these four foundations of mindfulness for six years . . . five years . . . four years . . . three years . . . two years . . . one year . . . seven

months . . . six months . . . five months . . . four months . . .
three months . . . two months . . . one month . . . or for half-a-
month, one of two results may be expected in him: knowledge
here and now, or if there be yet an element of clinging, non-return.

Let alone half-a-month, monks, were a monk to develop these
four foundations of mindfulness in this manner for seven days,
one of two results may be expected in him: knowledge here and
now, or, if there be yet an element of clinging, non-return.

That is why it was said thus, monks, the sole way of purity
for beings, for overcoming sorrow and misery, for destroying pain
and grief, for finding the right path, and of realizing Nibbāna,
is this road, that is to say, the four foundations of mindfulness.

The Buddha said this and the monks rejoicing, welcomed the
words of the Buddha.

Satipaṭṭhānasutta (Abridged), *Majjhimanikāya*, I, pp. 55–63; *Dīghanikāya*
II, pp. 291–315.

The Layman's Ethical Code

Thus have I heard:

Once the Buddha was staying in the Bamboo Grove, the Squirrels' Sanctuary, near Rājagaha.

At that time, young Sigāla, a householder's son, rising early in the morning, went forth from Rājagaha, with wet garments and wet hair, worshipped with joined hands the various quarters, namely—the east, the south, the west, the north, the nadir and the zénith.

Then the Buddha, having robed himself in the morning, took bowl and robe and entered Rājagaha for alms. Seeing young Sigāla worshipping he spoke to him saying:

'Why do you, young householder, worship in this manner?'

'Sir, my father, when he was dying, said to me: "Dear son, you should worship the quarters of the earth and sky." So I, Sir, respecting, revering, reverencing and honouring my father's words, rise early in the morning, and leaving Rājagaha, with wet garments and wet hair, worship these six quarters in this manner.'

'This is not the way, young householder, the six quarters should be worshipped in the discipline of the noble.'

'How then, Lord, should the six quarters be worshipped in the discipline of the noble? It would be an excellent thing, Sir, if you would teach me the doctrine according to which the six quarters should be worshipped in the discipline of the noble.'

'Well, young householder, listen and bear it well in mind; I will speak.' 'Very good, Sir,' responded young Sigāla.

The Buddha spoke as follows:

'Inasmuch, young householder, as the noble disciple (1) has put away the four vices in conduct, (2) inasmuch as he commits no evil action from four motives, (3) inasmuch as he does not pursue the six channels for dissipating wealth, he thus, avoiding these fourteen evil things, is a coverer of the six quarters, and enters the path leading to victory in both worlds: he is favoured in this world and in the world beyond. Upon the dissolution of the body, after death, he is born in a happy realm.

(1) What are the four vices in conduct that he has put away? The destruction of life, householder, is a vice and so are stealing, sexual misconduct, and lying. These are the four vices that he has put away.

(2) By which four motives does one commit no evil action? Evil deeds are done from motives of partiality, enmity, stupidity and fear.

But inasmuch as the noble disciple is not led by these motives, he through them does no evil deed.

(3) What are the six channels for dissipating wealth which he does not pursue? (*a*) Indulgence in intoxicants which causes infatuation and heedlessness, (*b*) sauntering in streets at unseemly hours, (*c*) frequenting degrading shows, (*d*) indulgence in gambling which causes heedlessness, (*e*) association with evil companions, (*f*) habitual idleness.

(*a*) There are, young householder, these six evil consequences in indulging in intoxicants which cause infatuation and heedlessness: (i) visible loss of wealth, (ii) increase of quarrels, (iii) susceptibility to disease, (iv) earning an evil reputation, (v) indecent exposure of the person, (vi) weakening of the intellect.

(*b*) There are, young householder, these six evil consequences in sauntering in streets at unseemly hours: (i) he himself is unprotected and unguarded, (ii) so also his wife and children, (iii) so also his property, (iv) he is suspected of criminal activities, (v) he is subject to false rumours, (iv) he meets with many troubles.

(*c*) There are, young householder, these six evil consequences in frequenting degrading shows: He is ever thinking: (i) where is there dancing? (ii) where is there singing? (iii) where is there music? (iv) where is there recitation? (v) where is there playing with cymbals? (vi) where is there pot-blowing?[1]

(*d*) There are, young householder, these six evil consequences in indulging in gambling: (i) the winner begets hatred, (ii) the loser grieves for lost wealth, (iii) visible loss of wealth, (iv) his word has no weight in a court of law, (v) he is despised by his friends and officials, (vi) he is not sought after for matrimony, for people would say that he is a gambler and is not fit to look after a wife.

(*e*) There are, young householder, these six evil consequences in associating with evil companions, namely: any gambler, any libertine, any tippler, any swindler, any cheat, any rowdy is his friend and companion.

(*f*) There are, young householder, these six evil consequences in being addicted to habitual idleness: He does no work, saying that (i) it is extremely cold, (ii) it is extremely hot, (iii) it is too late in the evening, (iv) it is too early in the morning, (v) he is extremely hungry, (vi) he is too full.

Living in this way, he leaves many duties undone, new wealth he does not acquire and wealth he has acquired dwindles away.'

The Master further said:

'One is a bottle friend; one says, "dear friend, dear friend", only to one's face; one is a friend and an associate only when in the hour of need.

Sleeping when the sun has risen, adultery, irascibility, malevolence, friendship with wicked men, avarice—these six causes ruin a man.

The man who has evil comrades and friends, is given to evil ways, to ruin does he fall in both worlds—here and hereafter.

---

[1] A form of amusement in ancient India.

Dice, women, liquor, dancing, singing, sleeping by day, sauntering at unseemly hours, evil companions, avarice—these six causes ruin a man.

Who plays with dice and drinks intoxicants, goes to women who are dear unto others as their own lives, associates with the mean and not with the wise—he declines just as the moon during the waning half.

The tippler of liquor who is poor, destitute, still thirsty whilst drinking, frequents the bar, sinks in debt as a stone in water, swiftly brings discredit upon his family.

Who by habit sleeps by day, and keeps late hours, is ever intoxicated, and is licentious, is not fit to lead a household life.

Who says it is too hot, too cold, too late, and leaves things undone, the opportunities for good go past such men.

But he who does not regard cold or heat any more than a blade of grass and who does his duties manfully, does not fall away from happiness.

These four, young householder, should be understood as foes in the guise of friends: (1) he who appropriates a friend's possessions, (2) he who renders lip-service, (3) he who flatters, (4) he who brings ruin.

(1) In four ways, young householder, should one who appropriates be understood as a foe in the guise of a friend: (i) he appropriates his friend's wealth, (ii) he gives little and asks much, (iii) he does his duty out of fear, (iv) he pursues his own interest.

(2) In four ways, young householder, should one who renders lip-service be understood as a foe in the guise of a friend: (i) he makes friendly profession as regards the past, (ii) he makes friendly profession as regards the future, (iii) he tries to gain your favour by empty sayings, (iv) when opportunity for service has arisen, he expresses his inability.

(3) In four ways, young householder, should one who flatters be understood as a foe in the guise of a friend: (i) he approves of his friend's evil deeds, (ii) he disapproves of his

103

friend's good deeds, (iii) he praises him in his presence, (iv) he speaks ill of him in his absence.

(4) In four ways, young householder, should one who brings ruin be understood as a foe in the guise of a friend: (i) he is a companion, when you indulge in intoxicants that cause infatuation and heedlessness, (ii) when you saunter in streets at unseemly hours, (iii) when you frequent degrading shows, (iv) when you indulge in gambling which causes heedlessness.

These four, young householder, should be understood as warm-hearted, real friends: (1) he who is a helper, (2) he who is the same in happiness and adversity, (3) he who gives good counsel, (4) he who sympathizes.

(1) In four ways, young householder, should a helper be understood as a warm-hearted, real friend: (i) he guards you, when you are heedless, (ii) he protects your property when you are heedless, (iii) he becomes a refuge when you are in danger, (iv) when you have commitments he provides you with double the supply needed.

(2) In four ways, young householder, should one who is the same in happiness and sorrow be understood as a warm-hearted, real friend: (i) his secrets he reveals to you, (ii) he conceals your secrets, (iii) in misfortune he does not forsake you, (iv) he sacrifices even his life for your sake.

(3) In four ways, young householder, should one who gives good counsel be understood as a warm-hearted, real friend: (i) he restrains you from doing evil, (ii) he encourages you to do good, (iii) he informs you of that which is unknown to you, (iv) he points out to you the path to a place of happiness.

(4) In four ways, young householder, should one who sympathizes be understood as a warm-hearted, real friend: (i) he does not rejoice in your misfortune, (ii) he rejoices in your prosperity, (iii) he restrains others speaking ill of you, (iv) he praises those who speak well of you.

And how young householder, does a noble disciple cover the six quarters?

The following should be looked upon as the six quarters. The parents should be looked upon as the east, teachers as the south, wife and children as the west, friends and associates as the north, servants and employees as the nadir, religious teachers and priests as the zenith.

In five ways, young householder, a child should minister to his parents as the east: (i) Having been supported by them I will now be their support, (ii) I will perform their duties incumbent on them, (iii) I will keep up the lineage and family traditions, (iv) I will make myself worthy of my heritage, (v) furthermore I will offer alms in honour of my departed relatives.

In five ways, young householder, the parents thus ministered to as the east by their children show their compassion: they (i) dissuade them from what is bad, (ii) persuade them to do good, (iii) get them properly educated, (iv) see them married at the proper age, (v) at the proper time they hand over their inheritance to them.

In these five ways do children minister to their parents as the east and the parents show their compassion to their children. Thus is the east covered by them and made safe and secure.

In five ways, young householder, a pupil should minister to a teacher as the south: (i) by rising from the seat in salutation, (ii) by attending on him, (iii) by listening to his instructions with attention and due reverence, (iv) by personal service, (v) receiving instructions respectfully.

In five ways, young householder, do teachers thus ministered to as the south by their pupils show their compassion: (i) they train them in the best discipline, (ii) they see that they grasp their lessons well, (iii) they instruct them in the arts and sciences, (iv) they introduce them to their friends and associates, (v) they provide for their safety in every quarter.

The teachers thus ministered to as the south by their pupils show their compassion towards them in these five ways. Thus is the south covered by them and made safe and secure.

In five ways, young householder, should a wife as the west be ministered to by a husband: (i) by being very courteous to her, (ii) by not despising her in any way, (iii) by being faithful to her, (iv) by handing over authority of domestic management to her, (v) by providing her with adornments.

The wife thus ministered to as the west by her husband shows her compassion to her husband in five ways: (i) she performs her household duties earnestly, (ii) she is hospitable to the kith and kin of her husband, (iii) she remains strictly faithful, (iv) she protects his earnings, (v) she is skilled and industrious in discharging her duties.

In these five ways does the wife show her compassion to her husband who ministers to her as the west. Thus is the west covered by him and made safe and secure.

In five ways, young householder, should one minister to his friends and associates as the north: (i) by liberality, (ii) by courteous speech, (iii) by being helpful, (iv) by being impartial, (v) by sincerity.

The friends and associates thus ministered to as the north by one show compassion to him in five ways: (i) They protect him when he is heedless, (ii) they protect his property when he is heedless, (iii) they become a refuge when he is in danger, (iv) they do not forsake him in his troubles, (v) they show consideration for his family.

The friends and associates thus ministered to as the north by one show their compassion towards him in these five ways. Thus is the north covered by him and made safe and secure.

In five ways should a master minister to his servants and employees as the nadir: (i) by assigning them work according to their ability, (ii) by supplying them with food and wages, (iii) by tending them in sickness, (iv) by sharing with them any profits. (v) by granting them leave and special allowances.

The servants and employees thus ministered to as the nadir by their master show their compassion to him in five ways: (i) they rise from their beds before the master, (ii) they go to sleep after him, (iii) they take only what is given, (iv) they perform their duties to the highest satisfaction, (v) they spread his good name and fame.

The servants and employees thus ministered to as the nadir show their compassion towards him in these five ways. Thus is the nadir covered by him and made safe and secure.

In five ways, young householder, should a householder minister to ascetics and Brahmins as the zenith: (i) by lovable deeds (ii) by lovable words, (iii) by lovable thoughts, (iv) by keeping open house to them, (v) by supplying their material needs.

The religious teachers and priests thus ministered to as the zenith by a householder show their compassion towards him in six ways: (i) they restrain him from evil, (ii) they persuade him to do good, (iii) they love him with a kind heart, (iv) they make him hear what he has not heard, (v) they clarify what he has already heard, (vi) they point out the path to a heavenly state.

In these six ways do ascetics and Brahmins show their compassion towards a householder who ministers to them as the zenith. Thus is the zenith covered by him and made safe and secure.'

When the Buddha had spoken thus, Sigāla, the young householder, said as follows:

'Excellent, Sir, excellent! It is as if, Sir, a man were to set upright that which was overturned, or were to reveal that which was hidden, or were to point out the way to one who had gone astray, or were to hold a lamp amidst the darkness so that those who have eyes may see. Even so, has the doctrine been explained in various ways by the Buddha.

I take refuge, Sir, in the Buddha, the Doctrine, and the Order. May the Buddha receive me as a follower; as one who has taken refuge from this very day to life's end.'

Sigālovāda Sutta (Abridged), *Dīghanikāya* III, pp. 180–93.

The Laity's Conduct

Now I will tell you of the life which a householder should lead, of the manner in which a disciple should conduct himself well. Monks' rules cannot be fulfilled by one who has a family.

Having refrained from oppressing all living beings in the world, whether strong or weak, let him not destroy life, nor cause others to destroy life and also not approve of others killing.

The disciple then, knowing that something belongs to others, should avoid stealing anything from any place; let him not cause others to steal, nor approve of others stealing; all stealing should be avoided.

The wise man should avoid an unchaste life as if it were a burning pit of live coals. If he is unable to lead a chaste life, let him not, at least, transgress with another's wife.

One should not tell lies to another whether in a public place or in an assembly. Let him not cause others to tell lies, nor approve of others telling lies. All sorts of falsehood should be avoided.

The householder, who delights in the Law, knowing that drinking intoxicants ends in madness, should not drink, nor should he cause others to drink and also not approve of others drinking.

The foolish commit evils in consequence of drunkeness and also make other people intoxicated. One should avoid this vice, the cause of demerit, insanity, delusion, a pleasure to the fool.

He should support his mother and father in a proper manner, and should practise a just trade.

Dhammika Sutta (Abridged), *Suttanipāta*, vv. 393-404.

Thirty-eight Blessings of Life

1. To dissociate with the wicked, 2. Association with the wise, 3. Honouring those worthy of being honoured, 4. Living in congenial surroundings, 5. To have performed meritorious deeds in the past, 6. To establish oneself on the right course, 7. To have extensive learning, 8. Knowledge of the arts and sciences, 9. Well-regulated discipline, 10. Well-spoken speech, 11. Succouring of mother, 12. Succouring of father, 13. Cherishing of wife and children, 14. Suitable occupation, 15. Generosity, 16. A purified life, 17. Rendering aid to relations, 18. To perform blameless deeds, 19. Abstaining from evils and avoiding them, 20. Total abstinence from intoxicating drinks, 21. Perseverence in virtuous acts, 22. Reverence towards those who are to be revered, 23. Humility, 24. Contentment, 25. Gratitude, 26. Calling attention to good advice on due occasions, 27. Patience, 28. Obedience, 29. To meet those who have subdued their passions, 30. Religious discussions at the right time, 31. Self-control, 32. Chastity, 33. Discernment of the noble truths, 34. Realization of Nibbāna, 35. Equanimity whilst beset by worldly contingencies, 36. Sorrowlessness, 37. Freedom from passion, 38. Security from sensual bindings.

Mahāmaṅgala Sutta (Abridged), *Suttanipāta*, vv. 258–68; *Khuddakapātha*, p. 3.

One's Downfall

He who adheres to the Law progresses; he who is averse to it, falls.

One who loves the company of the vicious, with the virtuous he finds no delight, he prefers the doctrine of the wicked—this is the cause of one's downfall.

Being fond of sleep, fond of garrulity, not industrious, and irritable—this is a cause of one's downfall.

Even when he is rich enough, he does not support his father and mother who are old and past their youth—this is a cause of one's downfall.

To deceive by falsehood a priest or ascetic or any other mendicant—this is a cause of one's downfall.

Having much wealth and ample gold and food one enjoys them alone—this is a cause of one's downfall.

If a man were to be conceited by his high ancestry and look down upon his own kith and kin—this is a cause of one's downfall.

To be a rake, a drunkard, a gambler, and to squander all one earns—this is a cause of one's downfall.

Not to be contented with one's wife, and to be seen with harlots and the wives of others—this is a cause of one's downfall.

Being past one's youth, to take a young wife and to be unable to sleep for jealousy of her—this is a cause of one's downfall.

To place in authority a woman given to drink and squandering, or a man of like behaviour—this is a cause of one's downfall.

If a member of a royal family, with vast ambition and of slender means, aims to be king—this is a cause of one's downfall.

Parābhava Sutta (Abridged), *Suttanipāta*, vv. 92–114.

Conditions of Prosperity

Once the Buddha was dwelling amongst the Koliyans at their market town called Kakkarapatta. There 'Longknee Tigerfoot', a Koliyan, approached the Buddha and, after greeting him, sat down at one side. So seated, he spoke thus to the Buddha:

'We, Sir, are laymen immersed in the round of worldly pleasure. We lead a life encumbered by wife and children. We delight in the muslins and sandalwood from Benares. We deck ourselves with garlands, perfume and unguents. We enjoy the use of both gold and silver. To those such as us, O Sir, let the Exalted One preach the Doctrine, teach those things that lead to weal and happiness in this life and to weal and happiness in the world to come.'

Four conditions, 'Tigerfoot', conduce to a householder's weal and happiness in this very life. What four?

Persistent effort, protecting one's own earnings, good friendship, and balanced livelihood.

What is persistent effort?

Herein, 'Tigerfoot', by whatsoever activity a householder earns his living, whether by farming, by trading, by cattle-herding, by archery, by government service, or by any other kind of craft—at that he becomes skilful and is not lazy. He is endowed with the power of discernment as to the proper ways and means; he is able to carry out his allocated duties. This is called persistent effort.

What is protecting one's own earnings?

Herein, 'Tigerfoot', whatsoever wealth a householder is in possession of, obtained by dint of effort, justly acquired by right means—such he husbands well by guarding and watching so that the government would not confiscate it, thieves would not steal, fire would not burn, water would not carry away, nor ill-disposed heirs remove. This is protecting one's own earnings.

What is good friendship?

Herein, 'Tigerfoot', in whatsoever village or market town a householder dwells, he associates, converses, engages in discussions with householders or householders' sons, whether young and highly cultured or old and highly cultured, full of confidence, virtue, charity and wisdom. He acts in accordance with the confidence of the confident, with the virtue of the virtuous, with the charity of the charitable, with the wisdom of the wise. This is called good friendship.

What is balanced livelihood?

Herein, 'Tigerfoot', a householder knowing his income and expenses leads a balanced life, neither extravagant nor miserly, knowing that thus his income will stand in excess of his expenses, but not his expenses of his income.

Just as one who weighs, or an apprentice of his knows, on holding up a balance, that by so much it has dipped down, by so much it has tilted up; even so a householder, knowing his income and expenses leads a balanced life, neither extravagant nor miserly, knowing that thus his income will stand in excess of his expenses, but not his expenses in excess of his income.

If, 'Tigerfoot', a householder with little income were to lead an extravagant life.

If, 'Tigerfoot', a householder with a large income were to lead a wretched life, rumour will say of him—'This person will die like a starveling'.

'Tigerfoot', the four channels for flowing away of amassed wealth are these: (i) debauchery, (ii) drunkenness, (iii) gambling, (iv) friendship, companionship and intimacy with evil doers.

Just as in the case of a great tank with four inlets and outlets, if a man should close the inlets and open the outlets and there should be no adequate rainfall, decrease of water is to be expected in that tank, and not an increase; even so there are four sources for the destruction of amassed wealth—debauchery, drunkenness, gambling, and friendship, companionship and intimacy with evil doers.

There are four sources for the increase of amassed wealth: (i) abstinence from debauchery, (ii) abstinence from drunkenness, (iii) non-indulgence in gambling, (iv) friendship, companionship and intimacy with the good.

Just as in the case of a great tank with four inlets and four outlets, if a person were to open the inlets and close the outlets, and there should also be adequate rainfall, an increase of water is certainly to be expected in that tank and not a decrease, even so these four conditions are the sources of increase of amassed wealth.

These four conditions, 'Tigerfoot', are conducive to a householder's weal and happiness in this very life.

Four conditions, 'Tigerfoot', conduce to a householder's weal and happiness in his future life. What four?

The accomplishments of confidence, virtue, charity and wisdom.

What is the accomplishment of confidence?

Herein a householder is possessed of confidence (based on knowledge), he believes in the Enlightenment of the Buddha: thus, indeed, is the Fortunate One, the Worthy One, the Fully Enlightened One, the Perfect One in Knowledge and Conduct, the Happy One, the Knower of the Worlds, the Guide of unruly men, the Teacher of gods and men, the Buddha. This is called the accomplishment of confidence.

What is the accomplishment of virtue?

Herein a householder abstains from killing, stealing, sexual misconduct, lying, and from intoxicants and drugs that cause infatuation and heedlessness. This is called the accomplishment of virtue.

What is the accomplishment of charity?

Herein a householder dwells at home with heart free from the stain of avarice, devoted to charity, open-handed, delighting in generosity, attending to the needy, delighting in the distribution of alms. This is called the accomplishment of charity.

What is the accomplishment of wisdom?

Herein a householder is wise: he is endowed with the wisdom that understands the arising and ceasing (of the five aggregates of existence); he is possessed of the noble penetrating insight that leads to the destruction of suffering. This is called the accomplishment of wisdom.

These four conditions, 'Tigerfoot', conduce to a householder's weal and happiness in his future life.

Vyagghapajja Sutta (Abridged), *Aṅguttaranikāya*, Vol. iv, pp. 281-5.

Paṭiccasamuppāda
(Dependent Origination)

In order of arising:

1–2. Conditioned by Ignorance Intentional activities arise;
3. Conditioned by Intentional activities re-linking Consciousness arises;
4. Conditioned by re-linking Consciousness Mind and Matter arise;
5. Conditioned by Mind and Matter the Sixfold base arises;
6. Conditioned by the Sixfold base Contact arises;
7. Conditioned by Contact Feeling arises;
8. Conditioned by Feeling Craving arises;
9. Conditioned by Craving Grasping arises;
10. Conditioned by Grasping Becoming arises;
11. Conditioned by Becoming Birth arises;
12. Conditioned by Birth ageing, death, sorrow, lamentation, pain, grief, and despair arise. Thus does this entire aggregation of suffering arise.

In order of cessation:

1–2. With the entire cessation of this Ignorance Intentional activities cease;
3. With the cessation of Intentional activities re-linking Consciousness ceases;
4. With the cessation of re-linking Consciousness Mind and Matter cease;
5. With the cessation of Mind and Matter the Sixfold base ceases;
6. With the cessation of the Sixfold base Contact ceases;
7. With the cessation of Contact Feeling ceases;
8. With the cessation of Feeling Craving ceases;
9. With the cessation of Craving Grasping ceases;
10. With the cessation of Grasping Becoming ceases;

11. With the cessation of Becoming Birth ceases;
12. With the cessation of Birth ageing, death, sorrow, lamentation, pain, grief and despair cease. Thus does the cessation of this entire aggregation of suffering result.

Vinayapiṭaka (Mahāvagga), Vol. I, p. 2; *Majjhimanikāya*, Vol. III, p. 63 f.

Gleanings from the Dhammapada

The *Dhammapada* is one of the important Buddhist texts which is widely used throughout the world. Preciseness of the utterances in this book is a remarkable feature. This book, containing the central message of the Buddha, occupies a unique position in Buddhism. Herein I present a simple condensation of the *Dhammapada* under different headings, dealing with some aspects of the Buddha's teaching. (*The numbers in brackets denote the numbers of the stanzas in the text.*)

Mental Control

(1) All conditions have mind as their forerunner, chieftained by the mind, they are mind-made. If one speaks or acts with a defiled mind unhappiness follows him, even as the wheel follows the foot of the drawer.

(2) If one speaks or acts with a pure mind happiness follows him, like a shadow that never leaves him.

(35) To control the mind is good.

(36) Let the wise man guard his mind. The guarded mind brings happiness.

(42) Whatever an enemy may do to an enemy, whatever a hater may do to a hater, a wrongly-directed mind will do us greater harm.

(43) Neither mother nor father, nor any other relative will do so much as does the well-directed mind.

Peace

(3) In those who harbour such thoughts: he abused me, he struck me, he overcame me, he robbed me—hatred never ceases.

(4) In those who do not harbour such thoughts hatred will cease.

(5) Hatred never ceases by hatred in this world. Through non-enmity it comes to an end. This is an ancient law.

(6) Some do not think that all of us here one day will die; if they did their dissensions would cease at once.

(221) One should give up anger, renounce pride.

(223) Let a man overcome anger by loving kindness; let him overcome evil by good, let him overcome miserliness by liberality, let him overcome the liar by truth.

(224) One should speak the truth, not give way to anger.

(227) There is none in the world who is not blamed.

(232) One should guard against misdeeds caused by speech. Let him practise restraint of speech. Let him practise virtue with his mind.

(234) The wise who control their body, speech and mind are indeed well controlled.

Self-discipline

(157) If one holds himself dear to himself, let him diligently watch himself.

(158) Let each man first establish himself in what is proper, then let him admonish others.

(160) One is the guardian of oneself; what other guardian could there be? With oneself fully controlled, one obtains a protector in him which is hard to obtain.

(165) A man defiles himself through his own evil actions; he purifies himself by avoiding evil. Purity and impurity depend on oneself. No one can purify another.

(166) Let no one neglect his own welfare for the sake of another's, however great.

(167) Do not follow mean things.

(168) Lead a righteous life.

(150) One should not regard the fault of others—things done and left undone by others. One should rather consider what by oneself is done and left undone.

(80) Irrigators lead the water wherever they like, fletchers shape shafts; carpenters carve the wood; the wise control themselves.

(183) The eschewing of all evil, the perfecting of good deeds, purifying of one's mind, this is the teaching of the Awakened One.

Happiness

(333) Happy is the practice of virtue during one's whole life; happy is confidence firmly rooted; happy is the attainment of wisdom; happy is the avoidance of evils.

(198) Let us remain unmoved in the midst of those who are moved by affliction.

(197) Let us live happily; hating none in the midst of those who hate.

(199) Let us be vigilant in the midst of those who are indolent.

(201) Conquest begets enmity; the defeated lie down in distress. The peaceful one lives happily giving up both victory and defeat.

(207) Association with the wise is happiness, like meeting with kinsfolk.

(204) Health is the highest gain; contentment is the greatest wealth; trusted is the best kinsman. Nibbāna is the supreme bliss.

Right company

(76) If a person sees a wise man who reproaches him for his faults, who shows what is to be avoided, he should follow such a wise man as he would a revealer of hidden treasures. It fares well and not ill with one who follows such a one.

(78) One should not associate with those who are evil-doers nor with persons who are despicable; associate with friends who are virtuous, associate with the best of men.

(81) As a solid rock is not shaken by the wind, so do wise men remain unmoved by praise or blame.

(328) If you find a companion, intelligent, one who associates with you, who leads a good life, lives soberly, overcoming all dangers, walk with him delighted and thoughtful.

(329) If you do not find such a companion, walk alone.

(330) It is better to live alone, there is no companionship with a fool.

(331) Companions are pleasant when an occasion arises; contentment is pleasant when mutual.

(332) To have the company of mother is happiness; to have the company of father also is happiness.

Moral rules

(246) Whosoever in this world destroys life, speaks untruth, takes

(247) what is not given to him, goes after the wives of others and gives himself to drinking intoxicating liquors, he even in this very life, ruins himself completely.

(239) Let a wise man remove the impurities of himself little by little.

(238) Make a refuge for yourself; strive quickly and be wise.

(238) Let not greed and wrong-doing bring you to grief.

The path

(273) The best path is the Eightfold path; the best truths are the Four Noble Truths; i.e.

(191) Suffering, its origin, its cessation and the path leading to its cessation.

(273) Enter upon this path.

Four Main Buddhist Traditions and their Allocation in the World

1. Theravāda—India, East Pakistan, Ceylon and South-East Asia.
2. Tibetan—India, Tibet, Nepal, Bhutan, Sikkim, Mongolia and Siberia.
3. Zen ⎫
4. Pure Land ⎬Japan, Korea, China, Viet-Nam, Malaysia and Singapore.

		POPULATION	BUDDHISTS
1. & 2.	India	437,324,983 (1961 census)	3,256,036
1.	Ceylon	10,582,064 (1963)	7,003,287
	Burma	23,390,000 (1968 est.)	21,051,000
	Thailand	26,257,916 (1960 census)	24,563,526
	Cambodia	6,300,000 (1968 est.)	6,237,000
	Laos	2,500,000 (est.)	2,475,000
	S. Viet-Nam	15,100,000 (1965 est.)	600,000
	East Pakistan	50,840,235 (1961 census)	373,867
2.	Tibet	1,000,000 (1967–8)	990,000
	Nepal	9,500,000 (1964 est.)	3,800,000
	Bhutan	750,000 (est.)	743,500
	Sikkim	162,189 (1961 census)	64,875
	Mongolia	1,120,000 (1966 est.)	1,010,000
	Siberia (Buriat, Kalmyk & Tuva Republics)		
		1,265,000 (1968 est.)	1,265,000
3. & 4.	Japan	100,160,000 (1967 est.)	78,770,000
	Korea	41,707,856 (1966 est.)	35,451,909
	China	700,000,000 (1968 est.)	300,000,000
	Viet-Nam	32,900,000 (1967 est.)	26,320,000
	Malaysia	10,020,800 (1967 est.) ⎫	3,000,000
	Singapore	1,955,600 (1967 est.) ⎭	
			516,975,000

The Main Festivals of Buddhism

Māgha Pūjā
> the full moon of February commemorating the Buddha's discourse to 1,250 fully enlightened monks in the form of three stanzas enshrining the essence of the Dhamma known as the *Ovādapātimokkha*.

Vesākha (Vesak)
> the full moon of May commemorating the birth, Enlightenment and final decease (*Parinibbāna*) of the Buddha.

Poson (or *Dhamma Vijaya* festival)
> the full moon of June commemorating the inception of Dhamma propagation, under Emperor Asoka of India, to foreign countries and particularly to Ceylon which was converted by his son, Mahinda.

Dhammacakka Day (or *Āsāḷha Pūjā*)
> the full moon of July commemorating the Buddha's First Sermon given at Benares.

MAHĀYĀNA COUNTRIES (FAR EAST ASIA)

April 8th
> the Buddha's birthday (in Japan, *Hanamatsuri*—'festival of flowers').

December 15th
> Enlightenment Day.

February 15th
> the *Mahāparinirvāṇa* of the Buddha.

The Four Sacred Shrines in India

Lumbinī (Rummindei, Nepal)
the birthplace of Gotama the Buddha.
Buddhagayā (Bodh-Gayā, Bihar):
the place where the Buddha attained Enlightenment.
Isipatana (Sarnath, near Benares or Varanasi, Uttar Pradesh)
the place where the Buddha preached his first sermon to the five disciples.
Kusinārā (Kusinagara, Uttar Pradesh):
the place where the Buddha passed away.

Chronological Table of Events in East and West

c. 560–480 BC	Gotama the Buddha.
c. 480	1st Council convenes to determine Pali Canon.
c. 380	2nd Council—secession of future adherents of the Mahāyāna.
274–236	Reign of Emperor Asoka who unifies India, is converted to Buddhism and popularizes the Dhamma by means of edicts on pillars, rocks and caves.
246	3rd Council: Sangha purified and initiation of missionary movement aimed at south, north and west. Mahinda, son of Asoka, takes Buddhism to Ceylon.
c. 80	4th Council—Pali Canon written on ola-leaves in Ceylon.
AC 67 & 217	Buddhism enters China.
c. 80	Council held in Kashmir under patron-king Kanishka.
150	Nagārjuna—great Mahāyāna philosopher—flourished.
372	Buddhism enters Korea.
420	Buddhaghosa—most renowned Theravāda commentator—flourished.
c. 430	Nālandā—most famous of all ancient Buddhist universities in India—begins activities.
400–500	Buddhism enters Burma, Cambodia, Viet-Nam and Indonesia.
c. 500	Ching-t'u (Pure Land school) established in China.
c. 520	Ch'an (Dhyāna-Jhāna-Meditation school) established in China by Bodhidharma.
522	Buddhism enters Japan and is later firmly established under Shōtoku Taishi (Regent).
c. 570	T'ien T'ai school founded in China by Chi-k'ai.

639   Buddhism enters Tibet.

600–700   Buddhism enters Thailand.

751   Buddhism firmly established in Tibet with the founding of the Nyingma-pa (school) under Padma Sambhava.

700–800   Buddhism established in Nepal, Bhutan and Sikkim.

804   Tendai school founded in Japan by Dengyo Daishi.

c. 810   Shingon school founded in Japan by Kobo Daishi.

1038–1122   Milarepa—Tibet's poet-ascetic-saint.

c. 1050   Kargyu-pa founded in Tibet by Mar-pa.

1071   Sakya-pa established in Tibet.

1175   Jodo shu (school) founded in Japan by Honen Shonin.

1191   Rinzai Zen shu introduced to Japan by Eisai.

1225   Soto Zen shu introduced to Japan by Dōgen. Jodo Shinshu founded in Japan by Shinran Shonin.

1253   Nichiren shu founded in Japan.

1261   Buddhism enters Mongolia and Siberia.

1300–1400   Buddhism established in Laos.

1409   Reformation in Tibet with founding of Gelug-pa by Tsongkha-pa—Dalai Lama becomes both Head of school and country.

1577   Buddhism firmly established in Mongolia.

1784–1842   Alexander Csoma de Körös—Hungarian traveller and collector of Tibetan manuscripts.

1832–1900   F. Max Mueller—Editor, *Sacred Books of the East*, which introduced Buddhism to the West in a comprehensive form.

1843–1922   T. W. Rhys Davids—greatest translator of Pali texts and founder of Pali Text Society, 1881, which has edited and translated virtually the whole of the Canon.

1862   First translation of *Dhammapada* into a Western language (German).

1864–1933   David Hewavitarne (later Anagārika Dharmapala)—leader of Buddhist revival in Ceylon and India.

1868–71   5th Council at Mandalay, Burma—Pali Canon inscribed on 729 marble slabs.

1878–1957   Nyānatiloka—first prominent (German) monk—ordained in Ceylon in 1903.

1879   Sir Edwin Arnold's *Light of Asia* published.

1880   Colonel Henry Steel Olcott, an American who worked for the upliftment of the Buddhists, arrived in Ceylon.

1891   The Maha Bodhi Society—oldest existing Buddhist society—founded in Colombo by Anagārika Dharmapala, branches later being established all over India and elsewhere.

Harvard Oriental Series founded by Henry Clarke Warren and Charles Rockwell Lanman which established Buddhism in the U.S.A. on a stable basis—55 volumes published to date.

1893   Parliament of Religions in Chicago—Buddhist impetus in the U.S.A. through Dharmapala, Paul Carus and C. T. Strauss.

1897   Bibliotheca Buddhica started by Sergei Oldenburg in Russia—30 volumes published to date.

1899   First Western monk—Gordon Douglas—ordained in Burma.

1903   First Buddhist society established in Germany under Karl Seidenstuecker.

1906   First Buddhist Congress in Europe convenes in Germany.

1907–23   First Buddhist society in Great Britain with Rhys Davids as President.

1908   First Sangha mission to West (England) led by Ananda Metteyya (Allen Bennet).

German Pali Society founded at Breslau.

1910   Monastic retreat created in Switzerland, near Lugano, for Nyānatiloka. Later, a second one was founded at Lausanne where the first novice in Europe was ordained.

1915   Tibetan Cathedral consecrated in Leningrad—Nicholas II officiates.

1920s   Revival of Buddhism in China under Ven. Tai Hsü.

1921   Future 'Old Buddhist Community' started in Bavaria by ex-judge George Grimm.

1924–8   'Das Buddhistische Haus' built in Berlin by Dr Paul Dahlke.

1924   The Buddhist Society, London, established by Christmas Humphreys.

Communist seizure in Mongolia—Buddhist monasteries later closed.

1926   British Mahābodhi Society founded by Dharmapala (revived 1966).

1928   'The Buddhist Mission' (London Buddhist Vihāra) established by Dharmapala.

1929   'Les Amis du Bouddhisme' formed in Paris under Constance Lounsbery.

1930   Sokagakkai—lay wing of the Nichiren Shōshu— founded in Japan by T. Makiguchi. By the 1960s it will have become the most formidable Buddhist movement in that country, claiming 15 per cent of the population and its own political party, the Komeito, No. 3 in the Diet.

1933   First European Congress held in Berlin.

1934   Second Congress held in London.

1937   Third Congress held in Paris.

1950   World Fellowship of Buddhists founded by Dr G. P. Malalasekera of Ceylon, permanent headquarters being established in Bangkok in 1963.

1951   'Buddhist Mission' started in Budapest, Hungary— first Buddhist centre in Eastern Europe.

1952   American nun, Dhammadinnā, gives impetus to Buddhist societies in Sydney, Melbourne and Brisbane (Australia).

1954   London Buddhist Vihāra re-opened.

Swedish Buddhist Society founded in Gothenburg (revived 1970).

1954–6   6th Council at Rangoon, Burma—Pali Canon revised and Pali edition published with Burmese translation.

1956   Buddha Jayanti Year commemorating 2,500 years of Buddhism.

Dr B. R. Ambedkar, father of the Indian Constitution, publicly embraces Buddhism together with 500,000 of his 'Untouchable' followers at Nagpur.

1957   'Das Buddhistische Haus' taken over by German Dhammadūta Society of Ceylon and converted into a monastery.

American Buddhist Academy opened in New York.

1958   First full Theravāda ordinations in the West—two Germans in the Royal Thai Embassy in London.

German Buddhist Union created.

Buddhist Publication Society established at Kandy, Ceylon, under the German monk, Nyānaponika—now foremost publishers of booklets in English.

1959   Buddhist Federation of Australia formed.

The Dalai Lama flees to India due to Chinese invasion.

1961   'Haus der Stille' meditation centre opened outside Hamburg.

First fascicule of Encyclopaedia of Buddhism published in Ceylon.

1962   Hampstead Buddhist Vihāra (now Wat Dhammapadīpa) opened in north London.

1963   Unified Buddhist Church established in South Viet-Nam—uniting the Mahāyāna and Theravāda schools and increasing the influence of Buddhism.

1963–8   Biddulph Meditation Centre in northern England.

1964   Johnstone House meditation centre opened in Scotland (converted into Samye-ling Tibetan Centre in 1967).

First (official) relic of the Buddha brought to the West and enshrined in the London Buddhist Vihāra.

1964 & 1967   Establishment of Sangha Sabhā (Council) of the U.K. under senior (Theravāda) monk, Ven. Dr H.

Saddhātissa (Head of the London Buddhist Vihāra since 1957).

1965 Wat Buddhapadīpa opened with Thai monks in south-west London.

1966 'Centre d'Etudes Bouddhique Ananda' opened in Brussels.

World Buddhist Sangha Sabhā formed in Ceylon in order to bring the Sanghas of the Mahāyāna and Theravāda closer together.

Buddhist centres established in Italy (Florence), East Germany (Halle University) and Canada (Toronto—temples existing only for Chinese and Japanese immigrants).

All Buddhist institutions in China finally closed following Communist 'Cultural Revolution'.

1967 Theravāda monasteries opened in Rio de Janeiro, Brazil (where only temples for 250,000 Japanese immigrants had existed) and Washington, D.C.

1968 Buddhist centre founded in Holland (The Hague). Activities of Buddhist Circle of Brno—the only active group in Czechoslovakia—curtailed following Russian invasion.

Buddhist shrine opened in Gilwell Park, the international training centre for Scouters, Essex, England. Meditation centre opened in Surrey.

First Zen temple in Europe consecrated at Gretz, France, and Tibetan Monastic Institute opened at Rikon, Switzerland.

Glossary

agape (Greek), a 'love feast', common meal of the early Christians

akusala, unwholesome, demerit, wrong, unskilful, unhealthy

ānāpānasati, mindfulness of in-and-out-breathing, a form of meditation

anattā (Skt. *anātman*), non-egoism, egolessness, selflessness, 'not self', 'not soul'

angst (German), anguish, fear, anxiety, disquiet, usually without obvious cause

anicca (Skt. *anitya*), impermanence, change, transiency of all phenomena arising due to conditioning factors

arahaṃ, free from all impurity, worthy one

caritas (Latin), 'high esteem', Christian charity, the love of God and one's neighbour, kindness

dāna, 'giving', practice of generosity, charity

deva, deity, celestial being, god

Dhamma (Skt. *Dharma*), teaching, doctrine, law, piety, etc.

dukkha, 'suffering', 'pain', 'sorrow', 'misery', 'unhappiness', 'unsubstantiality', 'dissatisfactoriness'

iddhi, psychic power

jhāna (Skt. *dhyāna*), a deep state of meditation, an experience reached in a certain order of mental states of meditation. It is divided into four such states

kamma (Skt. *karma*), volitional activity, lit. deed, consciously intended action

kasiṇa, external device to develop concentration of mind

kusala, wholesome, merit, right, skilful, healthy

maṇḍala, circle, disc, a mechanical aid to concentration

mettā (Skt. *maitri*), loving-kindness

Nibbāna (Skt. *Nirvāṇa*), an emancipation from all sorrows, extinction of all roots of evil, namely greed, hatred and delusion *nimitta*, 'sign', a mental 'image' arisen in the mind by successful meditation but appearing as if seen with the eye

paññā (Skt. *prajñā*), wisdom

paṭiccasamuppāda, dependent origination, conditioned genesis, causality

preta (Pali *peta*), 'gone', 'dead', departed spirit, 'shadow'

rāga, carnal 'thirst', lust, desire

saddhā (Skt. *sraddhā*), confidence, conviction

samādhi, higher meditation, mental culture

samatha, calmness, tranquillity, concentration

sammā ājīva, right means of livelihood

sammā diṭṭhi, right understanding or views

sammā kammanta, right action

sammā samādhi, right concentration

sammāsambuddho, completely enlightened by his own effort, the Fully Enlightened One

sammā saṇkappa, right thought or motive

sammā sati, right mindfulness

sammā vācā, right speech

sammā vāyāma, right effort

saṃsāra, continuity of existence, repeated birth, cycle of birth and death in material and immaterial abodes of beings

saṅgha, community of Buddhist monks

sati, mindfulness, awareness

satipaṭṭhāna, setting-up or foundation of mindfulness

satori (Japanese), spiritual achievement

sīla, morality, virtue

sutta (Skt. *sūtra*), discourse, sermon

Tisaraṇa, three refuges, three guides

Upanishad, knowledge gained at the feet of teacher, *Brahma*-knowledge by which ignorance is destroyed according to *Vedānta*

vihiṃsā, cruelty, violence, torture

vipāka, result, consequence, effect

vipassanā, 'seeing things in their true perspective', insight, analytical insight

vyāpāda, malevolence, ill-will, anger

Bibliography

Brewster, E. H., *The Life of Gotama the Buddha*, Routledge & Kegan Paul, London, 1956.

Burtt, E. A., *The Teaching of the Compassionate Buddha*, Mentor Religious Classic, New York, 1955.

Conze, Edward, *Buddhist Thought in India*, George Allen & Unwin, London, 1962.

Coomaraswamy, Ananda K., *Buddha and the Gospel of Buddhism*, Harper Torchbooks, New York, 1964.

Horner, I. B., *Milinda's Questions*, 2 vols., Pali Text Society, London, 1963–4.

Jayasuriya. W. F., *The Psychology and Philosophy of Buddhism*, Gunasena & Co., Colombo, 1963.

Jayatilleke, K. N., *Early Buddhist Theory of Knowledge*, George Allen & Unwin, London, 1963.

Jīvaka, Lobsang, *The Life of Milarepa*, John Murray, London, 1962.

Johannson, Rune, *The Psychology of Nirvāna*, George Allen & Unwin, London, 1969.

Khantipālo, Phra, *Tolerance, a Study from Buddhist Sources*, Rider & Co., London, 1964.

What is Buddhism? Social Science Association, Press of Thailand, 1965.

Ling, Trevor, *Buddhism*, Ward Lock Educational Ltd., London, 1970.

Nārada, Thera, *The Dhammapada* (trans.), John Murray, London, 1959.

Nyāṇaponika, Thera, *The Heart of Buddhist Meditation*, Rider & Co. (George Allen & Unwin), London, 1963.

Nyānatiloka, Mahāthera, *Buddhist Dictionary*, Island Hermitage Series, Colombo, 1956.

The Word of the Buddha, Buddhist Publication Society, Kandy, Ceylon, 1959.

Piyadassi, Thera, *The Buddha's Ancient Path*, Rider & Co. (George Allen & Unwin), London, 1963.

Rāhula, Walpola Sri, *What the Buddha Taught*, Second and enlarged edition, Gordon Fraser, Bedford, 1967.

Rhys Davids, T. W., *The Questions of King Milinda*, Dover Publications Inc., New York, 1963

Saddhatissa, H., *Handbook of Buddhists*, Mahabodhi Society, Sarnath, Benares, 1956.

Buddhist Ethics, George Allen & Unwin, London, 1970.

Sgam-po-pa, *The Jewel Ornament of Liberation*, Rider & Co. (George Allen & Unwin), London, 1959.

Suzuki, D. T., *Introduction to Zen Buddhism*, Philosophical Library, New York, 1949.

Thomas, E. J., *History of Buddhist Thought*, Routledge & Kegan Paul, London, 1933.

Woodward, F. L., *Some Sayings of the Buddha*, World Classics, Oxford, 1960.

Index